SILVERTON

THEN AND NOW
Revised Edition

*A Pictorial Journey Through Silverton, Colorado
1874 to 1922 and Beyond*

D1636985

By Allan G. Bird

ISBN 0-9619382-4-2

The Cover: The pen and ink drawing is the copyrighted
work of Michael Darr, Silver San Juan Gallery, Silverton,
Colorado.

**Allan G. Bird Publishing Co.
1135 Dudley St. Lakewood, Colorado 80215**

+ FOREWORD +

Today's Silverton visitor is treated to a timewarp of the American frontier beginning in 1874. Everything that one imagines of the old West happened here; gunfights, gambling, saloons, prostitution, all brought on by the lure of gold and silver. This book is an attempt to show the town as it originally was, along with the newsworthy items that happened in the early buildings. To give a complete history of each building would require a volume of abstracts that may be of interest to some but would probably tell the average reader more than he really wanted to know about Silverton. The writer has attempted to concentrate on old photos and newspaper stories. Few of the original buildings of old Silverton have survived. For a detailed history of the early pioneers, prior to 1883, the reader is referred to Allen Nossaman's excellent 400 plus page volumes entitled: *Many More Mountains- Vols. 1, 2, and 3*, Sundance Pub. Ltd. 1989-1998.

Before we begin our journey backward in time, a short orientation of the town of Silverton is necessary (Fig. 1). As one enters town from Ouray or Durango, the main street, known as Greene Street, bears slightly east of north. The train stops at the corner of Blair and 12th Streets. As you walk from the train along 12th toward the Grand Imperial Hotel, you are going toward the west. Reese Street is one block west of Greene Street and parallels Greene. A block beyond Reese is Snowden Street, also paralleling Greene. The four north-south streets mentioned are all named after the founding pioneers of Silverton: Tom Blair, George Greene, Dempsey Reese, and Francis Snowden. The street numbers increase toward the north. The Grand Imperial Hotel is on the northwest corner of 12th and Greene. As you turn right on Greene from 12th Street, you are headed toward 13th and 14th Streets. The Silverton Town Hall is on the southeast corner of 14th and Greene.

The reader should be aware that the racial standards of early Silverton would be considered unacceptable today. The views of the newspaper editors are apparent when the Chinese are pictured as "Pig-tailed, almond-eyed, celestials." The term "Dago" is often used when referring to the Italian population. The hatred of the Indians was never disguised. The prostitutes of Blair Street carried names like "Jew" Fanny, "Nigger" Lola, and "Sheeny" Pearl. At that time, the women used these names as trade names. The prostitutes seldom used their last names.

DEDICATION

To Norma

ACKNOWLEDGMENT

Many thanks to the fine people of Silverton who shared their memories and photographs of old Silverton. Many of those who contributed to the original 1990 version of this book are no longer with us. Hopefully, their memories will be preserved in this book.

I wish to express a special thanks to Duane Murphy, Curator of the San Juan County Historical Society Museum, without whose encouragement this book would not have been written.

Also, a special thanks to Allen Nossaman for his helpful conversations on Silverton history.

+ TABLE OF CONTENTS +

SILVERTON COLORADO

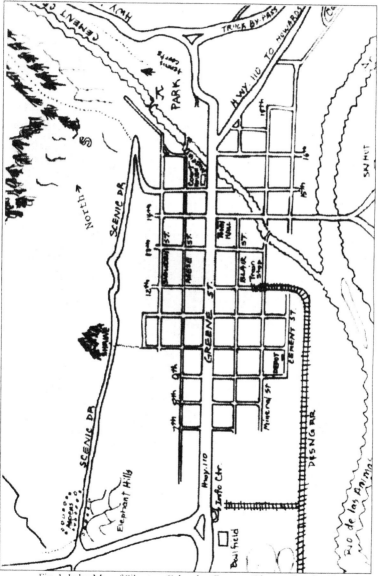

Fig. 1. Index Map of Silverton, Colorado. (Courtesy *Silverton Standard*)

+ CHAPTER 1 +

SILVERTON - THEN AND NOW   1874-1881

Much of the early history of Silverton between July 10, 1875, the date of the first issue of the *La Plata Miner*, and January 4, 1879, has been lost through the destruction of the early papers. Fortunately, the *Miner* published a brief history of early Silverton in 1877 and republished it in 1882. Letters from "old timers" also shed light on the early days of 1874-75. The Del Norte, Colorado, *San Juan Prospector*, often gave detailed accounts of happenings in Silverton during this period.

The first prospectors to enter the Silverton area were members of the ill-fated Baker Party. Charles Baker led a large group of gold seekers up the Animas Valley in 1860. One of the original members of the party wrote a brief description in the November 15, 1883, *San Juan Herald.* It read:

"There were 150 men in the original Baker Party. They reached Baker's Park (Silverton) in September and prospected about three weeks. The party scattered. Since then nothing definite has been heard from more than twelve of the old original Baker Party.
                    (Signed) Frank Koerle, member of original party."

Many members of the party froze to death; the Ute Indians killed others. Indians killed Baker a few years later. Only a small amount of gold was found at the mouth of Eureka Gulch, about seven miles north of Silverton near the ghost town of Eureka.

The Civil War ended prospecting for the next eleven years. In 1871, a party of prospectors led by George Howard, a member of the original Baker Party, entered the San Juans by way of Stony Pass from Del Norte, Colorado. Howard built his cabin at Howard's Fork, later Howardsville. Reese, Snowden, Blair, and others settled at the original campsite of the Baker Party, known as Baker's Park. None of the prospectors wintered over for the next three years. Reese, French, and others, discovered the Little Giant Mine in 1871. They took specimens of gold ore to Santa Fe, New Mexico, where they induced Gov.William Pile and some other Santa Fe parties to outfit prospectors to search for vein-type gold deposits. The bitter San Juan winters limited their prospecting time to the short summer months.

In 1872, no more than fifty persons were in camp. The following year, 1873, the group numbered one hundred. A small primitive stamp mill was packed in to process the Little Giant ores. Only a few thousand dollars worth of gold was realized during this season. The property showed a loss, almost ending the search for gold in the San Juans.

During the summer of 1873, the town site of Silverton was laid out. Before the Brunot Treaty of September 1873, the San Juans were owned by the Ute Indians led by Chief Ouray. All mining and property claims by the prospectors were illegal. In the spring of 1874, the surveys were made and the title to the town site was perfected. The original town company consisted of: George Greene & Co., Calder, Reuse & Co., Dempsey Reese, F. M. Snowden, W. Mullholand, K. Benson, N. E. Slaymaker, Thomas Blair, and Wm. Kerns. Most of these men remained in Silverton and sowed the seeds of the present town.

Fig. 2. **Then** - Col. F. M. Snowden's cabin. Photo taken April 11, 1891. (San Juan County Historical Society photo)

According to a story in the November 8, 1883, *San Juan Herald,* Tom Blair built the first cabin within the new town site on a lot now occupied by the Grand Imperial Hotel. Dempsey Reese erected a homestead cabin near the mouth of Cement Creek, north of town. Attorney N. E. Slaymaker built the second cabin on Reese Street. "Although a plain log cabin, it was considered by the rustic inhabitants an ornament to Chicago or New York City." Col. F. M. Snowden built a cabin on the northwest corner of Snowden and 13th Streets (Fig. 2). The inscription on an early photo described Snowden's cabin as the first cabin. In the

September 30, 1905, *Silverton Standard*, a brief article stated:

> John P. Johnson, the first real house builder at Silverton and Eureka, departed for New York this morning, probably never to return. Mr. Johnson was in Silverton country with Ed Clements and R. J. McNutt in 1871, and that year he built a house at Eureka, nine miles above Silverton. This was the first house built on the Animas River after the Baker party built a log cabin town in 1861 at the point where the old Baker Bridge now stands (near Durango). Mr. Johnson also built the second house, a log cabin in Baker's Park, where Silverton now stands. Mr. Clements vouches for this. Mr. Johnson says it is true, and doubtless Judge McNutt will corroborate, just to correct history.-Monday's *Durango Herald*.

It is questionable who built the first cabin. A member of the 1872 party wrote an excellent description of early Silverton. In the September 8, 1881, *San Juan Herald*, he wrote:

> It seems an age since the spring of '72. I have seen the rich become poor and the poor rich. I have seen men who never knew what it was like to have a dollar over and above the absolute expenses of life, amass a fortune in a day. I have seen men whose highest ambition was to swill whisky and gamble, to whom the society of prostitutes and their pimps was all sufficient, suddenly raised to wealth by some unexpected as well as undeserved stroke of fortune, and immediately be received into the society of the elite.
>
> Silverton's first winter (that of '74) was one ever to be remembered by those whose lot was cast amid the snowbound hills surrounding Baker's Park; for genial kindly feeling and sociability that winter has never been equaled, and never will be, in the metropolis of San Juan. Because we were few and isolated each and all tried to make the best of it, and as pleasant as possible for the rest. Our number of ladies was small but 'select': i.e., for their ladylike bearing, their good nature and sociability. They consisted of Mrs. W. E. Earl, Mrs. Cotton, Mrs. B. F. Holmes, Mrs. J. Lambert, Mrs. Eaton and daughter, Mrs. Edward Greene, Mrs. B. Harwood, and Mrs. H. L. Rogers, only a few of whom have continued to make Silverton their home.
>
> Dances (were) held at Greene & Company's store, and the debates in an old building where Tom Blair's saloon now stands and was afterwards used as a blacksmith shop (Greene Street, three doors north of 13th Street on west side of the Street). The buildings in town were few and far between. Greene's store and the building opposite (Fig. 3), occupied by Harwood and wife downstairs, and Greene and Earl families upstairs.

families upstairs. Snowden's and Rowland's cabins, adjoining on Snowden Street, Cotton's house (Fig. 4), the frame and log I have spoken of above; the log standing on the corner now occupied by Posey and Wingate's brick (Fig. 14), Reese's cabin upon Cement Creek, occupied by Ufford as county clerk, district court, and post office. This was one of the most important places that winter. Ufford had forty gallons of whisky left with him by Randall & Adsit, with instructions to sell, and as he could find no one else to sell to he sold to L. L. Ufford who kept open house for the boys during the winter. The whisky was all gone in the spring and Adsit received his pay in full.

Poor Greenelle, then sheriff, brought most of the mail for us that winter. We paid as high as fifty cents a letter for postage.

Signed 'ODE'

Greene started a sawmill in August 1874. Most of the early buildings were log cabins. The dwelling mentioned above that housed the Harwood, Earl, and Greene families, was of frame construction. It is the oldest surviving building in Silverton (Fig. 3). The second oldest surviving house, the Cotton House, was built of logs and later covered with siding (Fig. 4).

Figs 3 & 4. **Now**- Harwood-Earl-Greene House on the left. Built in 1874. Oldest surviving house in Silverton. Located between 14th and 15th Streets on the east side of Reese Street. The Cotton house is on the right. The second oldest house, built in 1874. Original log house has been covered with siding. Located on the southeast corner of 14th and Reese Streets. (Allan G. Bird photos-May, 1999)

John Curry, editor of Silverton's first newspaper, told of his arrival in Silverton on June 13, 1875:

> On June 12th we reached Howardsville, via Stony Pass. Foot sore and weary we plodded down Greene Street about 6 p.m., June 13th, to the corner now occupied by Posey & Wingate's brick block (Fig. 14) where was located a cabin with a roof of Aspen poles. In the cabin was located the county clerk's office.

Curry rented a small cabin, located where the south half of the Wyman Hotel now stands, and printed the first edition of the *La Plata Miner* on July 10, 1875. His first ads were for Greene & Company's store and R. C. Luesley's general merchandise store, next door to the north of the newspaper offices. He also ran ads for four attorneys. There were about twenty buildings in town when John Curry started his newspaper.

July, 1875 was an eventful month in Silverton. The first issue of Curry's paper announced the opening of the Rough and Ready Smelter. The paper stated that the smelter made "its first run, which also proved to be its last." One metric ton of bullion was produced. No mention was made of its value; the fact that it operated only one day speaks for itself. Many of the early merchants began business in July, 1875. At that time, Silverton did not have a central business district. Buildings were scattered between Reese and Greene Streets. B. A. Taft opened a drug store on the northwest corner of 13th and Reese Streets. After August, the post office was moved to a small cabin on the lot north of the present Teller House. Several saloons opened during the year. Dr. A. H. Kallenberg, who also ran an assaying business on the side, served the town. The paper stated that, "he was one of the finest physicians in the state."

The first baby was born on July 8, 1875, a girl, to Mr. and Mrs. B. P. Taft, half-brother to the druggist B. A. Taft.

Mrs. Earl and Miss Morton solicited money for the building that was to house the school. It was also used for the first church and town hall offices (Fig. 5).

Fig. 5. **Then** – Artist's 1877 sketch of Silverton. (Courtesy of the Denver Public Library Western History Department)

The first Fourth of July celebration attracted "a big crowd." The Saturday night prior to the Fourth was punctuated by one of the town's first shootings. A highly inebriated miner named W. Kelley, accidentally shot John Connor. Drs. Kallenberg and Cushing dressed the wounds. Since the town had no jail at this time, Kelley was chained to the floor of a slab cabin near R. J. Brun's furniture store (on the west side of Greene Street, between 14th and 15th Streets).

On August 15, 1875, the new Greene & Co. Smelter made a successful run under the management of J. A. Porter.

One must remember that until the arrival of the railroad in 1882, Silverton was almost inaccessible from the outside world. Pack trains and, later, primitive wagon toll roads provided access only during the summer months. During the winter months, only mail was packed in on foot, using snowshoes (long skis). Because of the long winter, John Curry's newspaper ran out of newsprint. John Reed, assisted by Mr. T. P. Plants, packed paper from Carr's cabin in Hinsdale County. Three bundles, weighing 50 pounds each, cost $140 delivered to Silverton.

In 1876, Silverton was described by an eyewitness as "presenting a rather disgusting appearance." After a long winter, the first pack train of burros arrived on May 6. The paper reported:

> It was a glad sight, after six long, weary months of imprisonment, to see the harbingers of better days, to see these messengers of trade and business, knowing that once more the road was opened to the outside world.

By 1876, the town consisted of 350 people, 100 houses, two saw mills, and four stores, along with the usual complement of saloons, hotels, boarding houses, cigar and tobacco shops, and gambling halls.

Our photographic journey begins in 1877. An artist's sketch, labeled Silverton, 1877 (Fig. 5), shows the town in the background with the Greene Smelter in the foreground. The ill-fated Rough & Ready Smelter is the farthest building toward the left. The two northernmost buildings on Reese Street are the original Harwood-Earl-Greene home on the east side and the old Greene General Store on the west side. The central business district was concentrated between 13th and 14th Streets on Greene Street.

Figure 6 is one of the oldest surviving photographs of individual businesses. This scene was taken looking north toward the present Silverton Town Hall (Fig. 7). The photo, Fig. 6, is dated as late July or August, 1877. The building on the far right is the Haines & McNicholas General Merchandise Store. Construction on the building began June 2, 1877. The store was opened in July. The firm dissolved sometime before or during early 1878, when Mickey Breen replaced Haines. The Meat Market was owned by the Ambold Brothers and was, according to the 1882 Official Directory, established in 1875. Next door is Fred Furrer's Barbershop. Note the barber poles painted along the side of the unpainted adjacent building. The San Juan Restaurant and Bakery occupied the large two-story frame north of the barbershop. The temporary sign says "Restaurant and Bakery." The restaurant operated until early 1879, when Montgomery & McNeil moved in with a general store. The building was built in 1877 and has not yet been painted. North of the San Juan Restaurant is a vacant lot. On the corner is the C. S. & N. Post Office Drug Store. The C. S. & N. stood for Chestnut, Stephens and Newman. Dr. H. S. Cowen M.D. had his office in the rear of this building. He later gave up the practice of medicine and took over the drug store. This was Silverton's first substantial post office. The store was opened July 18, 1877. Directly across the street stood Luesley's store, the first general store on Greene Street. In 1877, many of the lots on this block were occupied by businesses.

The year 1878 brought continued growth to the town. In June, Fred C. Sherwin and W. F. Knowlton leased John B. Rowland's cabin (on the northeast corner of 13th and Greene Streets), and established a general merchandise store. Two years later, they constructed Silverton's first stone building (which is today occupied by the Pickle Barrel Restaurant) (Figs. 8 & 9).

Across the street a block to the north, stood the Silverton Hotel. The original log hotel was built by J. L. Briggs in 1875 and was known as the Briggs House. Murphy and Henry bought the Briggs House on June 11, 1876, renaming it the Silverton Hotel. They expanded the building, making it one of the showcase hotels of Silverton. One of Silverton's earliest gun fights took place in the street in front of the Silverton Hotel (Figs. 10, 11). The story was preserved in the October 26, 1878, Del Norte *San Juan Prospector*. It seems that Tom Milligan and Bill Connors got into a fistfight over some trivial matter. Connors threatened to shoot Milligan on sight. Connors stepped out in front of the Silverton Hotel and discovered Milligan walking past the hotel. The two men spotted each other about the same time, both drawing their guns. Milligan got off the first shot, which hit Connors just above the navel, lodging in his intestines. Connors was crawling toward the hotel when Milligan got off two more shots, both missing. He was arrested and given a preliminary hearing the next day. The verdict was that the shooting was done in self-defense. Connors died an agonizing death three days after the shooting.

Aside from the above incident, Silverton was remarkably free from serious crime. In April, 1879, the paper complimented Marshal James Cart. He received a unanimous vote from the people of Silverton in the town election. The *Miner* wrote:

> Our town during the past summer was remarkably orderly for a mining camp, especially for the business center of the mining districts of southern Colorado and San Juan. The re-election of Mr. Cart is a guarantee of order and respect for the law this coming summer.

About two weeks after the above compliment, a new type of crime emerged in town - arson. Between the time of its founding and the fall of 1883, Silverton was without a central water system. All drinking water was hauled from a single spring owned by Mr. Luesley. The only fire protection was through a series of ditches running between the buildings and the dirt streets. The water was channeled from Cement Creek, north of town. The ditches were only usable during the summer

Fig. 6. **Then** - 1877 business houses on the east side of Greene Street, between 13th and 14th Streets in late summer. (Eddie Lorenzon photo)

Fig. 7. **Now** - Same scene as Fig. 6. Silverton City Hall is on the left. The 1901 Anderson Building is in the center of the photo. (Allan G. Bird photo-March, 1990)

months. It is a miracle that the entire town did not burn to the ground during the winter when the frame buildings were heated by primitive stoves and illuminated by candles and coal oil lanterns. Because of the seriousness of the situation, arson was a lynching offense. On Sunday night, the night of April 27, Silverton's first arson attack took place. To insure that the fire completed its job, the arsonist cut off water from the town ditches. The May 3 issue of *The Miner* read:

> Witnesses saw flames in the window of Breen and McNicholas (across the street). The Reese Hook and Ladder Company at one time gave up the corner store building. They tore down the old log building. After the water was reopened, those present were able to save the two adjoining buildings. The cabin destroyed was the property of R. C. Luesley, as was the store building on the corner (Luesley's 1875 store). Loss will not exceed $600. No insurance. Log building was built in 1875, and for one year was occupied as The *Miner* office. Fire was set on the north side, kindling wood used. No wind or would have been worse. Building of J. F. Cotton, just to the rear, would have been destroyed and the Silverton Hotel on the opposite corner would have been in great danger.
>
> A night watchman has been appointed by the Board of Trustees, and it is safe to say that should the incendiary be caught at his work in the future, his life will be worth the value of the rope, and that will be donated most cheerfully.

The *Miner* moved from the above building in July, 1876, almost a year from the date of their first issue. They relocated on the west side of Reese Street (about two doors north of B. A. Taft's Drug Store).

As mentioned earlier, the town water supply was delivered in a burro-drawn cart during the summer and by dog sled during the winter. The water man was a gent by the name of Frank Armine Schneider. The usual price for water was one cent per gallon. Schneider had the habit of beating his burro when the animal got a little balky. His neighbors and customers finally had enough of this foul treatment and had him arrested. He was taken before the Justice and fined $5 plus costs. He informed all those that witnessed against him that the cost of their water just increased to ten cents a gallon. He smiled as he left the courtroom saying: "I'll dry dem fellers up."

James Dermody, a hard-drinking Irishman, had, on the night of May 26, 1879, been on a spree at Jane Bowen's Westminster Hall (Fig. 28). Night watch Hiram Ward talked James and his brother, Pete, into going home and sleeping it off. The next night, May 27, Ward again encountered the pair in Goode's Senate Saloon, both blind drunk. He told them to go home. James told Ward to mind his own business. Ward forced James out the front door and a scuffle ensued. Dermody bit Ward on the finger and got a hammerlock around Ward's neck, forcing him into the ditch in front of the saloon. Flat on his back, with both brothers ganging up on him, Ward pulled his gun and shot James, inflicting a mortal wound. When he was

Fig. 8. **Then - 1885.** View of the east side of Greene Street, between 13th and 14th Streets showing the 1880 Sherwin stone store (present day Pickle Barrel Restaurant), (Eddie Lorenzon Collection)

Fig. 9. **Now -** View of Fig. 8. Smedley's Ice Cream Parlor, built in the 1970s, is next to the old Sherwin stone building (Pickle Barrel Restaurant). (Allan G. Bird photo-May, 1999)

Fig. 10. **Then** - 1883 street scene looking south along the west side of Greene Street from a point north of 14th Street. Old Silverton Hotel on right. Matthews & Walton's Store across the street. (Original 1875 Luesley's General Store). (Mrs. Ruth Gregory Collection)

Fig. 11. **Now**-View of approximately the same scene as Fig. 10. 1902 Wyman building (Wyman Hotel) is on the right. Silverton Hotel site was across the street, to the right of the Wyman building. Now a vacant lot on the corner. (Allan G. Bird photo-August, 1998)

sober, Dermody was a likable, friendly man. The papers claimed that it was a tragic, uncalled for, shooting. A coroner's jury found Ward innocent. Dermody was buried in Silverton's Hillside Cemetery. This shooting turned many of the local folks against Ward.

On August 23, 1879, the town was shocked by the news that James M. (Ten Die) Brown, one of the owners of Brown & Cort's Saloon, had been shot and killed. His saloon was located on Greene Street (next door to the north of Tom White's Olympic Saloon (Fig. 12). The large two-story stone and brick building (Fig. 14) now occupy this site. The issues of the Silverton paper reporting this event are missing, however the Del Norte *San Juan Prospector* of September 6, 1879 carried the story. They reported that on the night of August 26, two men by the name of Harry Cleary and "Mexican Joe" entered Brown & Cort's Saloon. After spending some time around the Faro table, Cleary, probably under the influence, tried to pick a fight with some of the customers. Brown told him to leave. Cleary threatened to whip Brown. As Brown escorted Cleary beyond the front door, Cleary pulled a gun and shot Brown. It was reported that he shot him through the heart and lung. Brown was able to fire ten shots at the fleeing Cleary. While he was shooting, night watchman Hiram Ward, who had only one arm, happened upon the scene. One of Brown's wild shots caught Ward in his left shoulder ranging downward, lodging near the spinal column. He returned the fire, inflicting a flesh wound on Brown. Brown died five minutes after the first shot.

Harry Cleary was arrested and lodged in jail. That night, between one and two o'clock in the morning, as the town marshal was on his way home, six masked men surrounded him with guns drawn demanding the keys to the jail. The marshal readily gave them the keys. He was told by the mob to go home and not return for one hour, on pain of death. The mob took Cleary, gagged him, tied his hands behind him, (his feet were already shackled), threw a rope around his neck, pushed him on his back, and dragged him about 300 yards down the alley to an ox-shoeing frame at the rear of the blacksmith shop. Here they hung him, leaving him to die of strangulation.

The marshal found the victim at 5 o'clock that morning. The reaction of the town was one of pleasure. They felt that Cleary would make a good example. The law, in the eyes of most, was too lenient and too slow. Unfortunately, as often happened in this situation, they probably lynched the wrong man. It seems that Brown was a member of the city council and had been trying to have Ward removed from his job as night watchman because of his physical handicap. It is doubtful that Brown would have been able to get off ten shots, one of which hit Ward, if Cleary's bullet had pierced his heart and lung. In all probability, Cleary's shot caused the flesh wound and Ward's shot caused the fatal wound. Ward stumbled onto the situation and took advantage of it to kill his enemy. Brown was probably aiming at Ward when Ward was shot. Ward was not expected to live at the time but he did survive.

Several years after the shooting, on September 23, 1883, the *La Plata Miner* printed the following story:

Most of our readers will remember H. W. Ward, who became famous in Silverton a few seasons ago about the time of the J. M. Brown tragedy, and will be edified to learn that somewhere in Ohio, he killed his brother-in-law and then himself. Fit ending to a record whose every page is marked by the stain of blood on his fellow man.

By April 1, 1880, Silverton had ten saloons, which contributed a total of $1880 to the town treasury for liquor licenses. About the middle of April, George Bayly and Dr. E. T. Pitman, both of Del Norte, bought the C. S. & N. Post Office Drug Store. In mid-June, the old log Sherwin and Houghton store disappeared and excavation began on the cellar and foundation of the stone building. (Today's Pickle Barrel Restaurant on the northeast corner of 13th and Greene Streets). The *Miner* reported:

> Sherwin & Houghton intend to place in the great San Juan country, a monument of enduring granite that will last for ages, and which will be a credit to the place, and an honor to the enterprising originators (Figs. 8, 9).

In November, the paper described the store as being:

> The best evidence of Silverton's prosperity and the confidence that our best businessmen have in our future. The counters in this store, some 90 feet in all, are very handsomely and substantially made and grained in black walnut, with French walnut trimmings, costing to make and finish over $1000. The store is neatly painted white, having French walnut trimmings, giving it a very elegant and finished appearance. We understand the entire interior outfit cost about $2500.

A few doors to the north of the Sherwin & Houghton building was located one of Silverton's earliest hotels. It was opened in the winter of 1875 and was built over two lots (50 feet) by Mr. I. E. Grout. It opened as the Centennial Hotel. On June 1, 1877, Grout leased the hotel to Capt. W. S. Walker and it became known as the Walker House. Walker later bought the Earl Hotel (on the southwest corner of 13th and Snowden Streets) and operated the second Walker House for many years. On January 1, 1879, Mr. B. Suydun leased the operation and renamed it the Grand Central Hotel. In April 1880, Capt. Walker sold the hotel to Tom Rockwood, a young man who had suffered a tragic personal loss less than a year earlier.

Rockwood married Sadie, the daughter of the hotel founder I. E. Grout, on September 24, 1878. On September 4, 1879, the couple had a baby girl. Nine days later, Sadie, 19 years old, died of childbirth complications. The baby lived. Tom Rockwood renamed the hotel the Rockwood House and had the grand opening June 26, 1880. Rockwood was having financial problems. The unpaid debts resulted in the hotel being closed by the sheriff on August 21, 1881. It had again been named the Grand Central Hotel. The 1881 photograph shows the building with the Grand Central Hotel sign in front (Fig. 12). In later years, the hotel was run as a boarding house. Saloons and restaurants occupied the two front stores on the main floor. At one time, someone opened the Poodle Dog Saloon, which lasted a very short

Fig 12. **Then**-1881 photo of Greene Street looking north from 13ᵗʰ Street. Brown & Cort's Saloon is the third building from the left. (Colo. Historical Society photo)

Fig 13. **Now**-Cole-Hoffman building. west side of Greene Street north of 13ᵗʰ Street. Brown & Cort's Saloon occupied the space now covered by the right half of the building. (Allan G. Bird photo-August 1998)

time. Not many rough and tough miners wanted to be caught drinking in the Poodle Dog Saloon.

Next door to the Grand Central Hotel was Eugene McCarthy's Star of the West Saloon, run by Knute Benson (Fig. 12). This saloon was built in 1875 and advertised as Silverton's oldest saloon. This meant that it was the oldest surviving saloon, as others were older. Both McCarthy and Benson acquired wealth through mining in later years. Benson built the large Benson Hotel building (on the northeast corner of 12th and Greene Streets) in 1902.

1880 marked the construction of the Posey & Wingate building (Fig. 14). Silverton's first large brick building. (This building survives today as a gift shop and restaurant.

Fig. 14. **Now**-May, 1999 photo showing the 1880 Posey & Wingate brick building on the southwest corner of 13th and Greene Streets. Silvertons first large brick building. The cast iron front was hauled over Stony Pass by mules. (Allan G. Bird photo)

The November 6, 1880, *La Plata Miner* reported:

The two-story brick on the southwest corner of Greene and 13th is 50 X 76 feet. First floor will be divided into two stores, the one on the corner to be occupied by the San Juan County Bank, and the other by Messrs. Posey & Wingate themselves, to carry on their extensive hardware business. They will have two entrances, one on Greene Street and one on 13th Street. The entire front of the building, up to the second story, is composed of solid cast iron (15,000 pounds hauled over Stony Pass). 200,000 bricks were used. The walls are four bricks thick.

The rear 24-foot frame addition to the present brick building was added a short time later. On October 10, 1880, brick replaced the frame front of the new building.

Silverton's first restaurant owner, Otis Ballou, moved his Animas Restaurant from Greene Street to a location on 13th Street, about two doors west of the alley separating the Posey & Wingate building from Reese Street. Ballou's Animas Restaurant was opened in 1875, just north of where the Pickle Barrel Restaurant now stands. No one knows what the name of the new restaurant was, but it was probably called the 13th Street or the Ballou Restaurant. In 1879, Ballou had the contract to feed the town prisoners at 40 cents per meal.

Robert Ambold built a frame meat market next door, to the east, of Ballou. There was a space of about ten feet between the buildings that Ballou filled in with a small Chinese laundry. Ambold was there only a short time when he leased the building to Sam Jones and John O'Neil, who opened what later became the Sunrise Saloon.

On October 2, 1880, Tom Blair, for whom Blair Street was named, opened the Rose Bud Saloon. He purchased the old blacksmith shop of Mr. Bush from Bush's wife, Bettie, for $825. After a short time, he moved the old shop to the rear of his new lot and built a new one-story structure for his Rose Bud Saloon. His saloon was located three doors north of the corner of 13th and Greene Street, on the west side of the street. Blair was one of the discoverers of the Aspen silver mine near Silverton. He sold his interest in the mine and proceeded to lose most of his stake in the saloon business. He was one of the founding fathers of Silverton and owned a large amount of Silverton real estate.

Where the Grand Imperial Hotel now stands, was a frame saloon owned by Anthony Miller. Miller also operated a saloon located three doors north of the hotel, (on the lot now occupied by the Rocky Mountain Gift Shop). Miller sold his land to the builders of the Thomson block (Grand Hotel) in 1882 for $3000 and retired. Next to Miller's lot, to the south, was a saloon known as "Jacks," operated by Pendleton & Hamlin. In the spring of 1881, they moved upstairs in the new Posey & Wingate brick building and opened the Metropolitan Billiard Hall and Saloon. Tom Blair owned the land on which this saloon was located and must have torn the building down or moved it before Thomson purchased the land as Blair sold two vacant lots to Thomson for $1. On the corner lot was a building used by Pearson's Meat Market. E. M. Johnson owned this land. On June 3, 1882, he sold to Thompson for $1600. Pearson's was one of the oldest businesses in Silverton. All of these buildings were torn down before the July 27, 1882, ground breaking for the Thomson block, which was to become the Grand Hotel (later the Imperial, and now the Grand Imperial-Figs. 15 & 16). No photographs exist of the original frame buildings that were on these lots.

The cornerstone for the Congregational church was laid on August 20, 1880, at

Fig. 15. **Then**-1883 engraving of the Grand Hotel (Now Grand Imperial Hotel). Corner store housed I. & M. Kruschke's Clothing Store, next was Kinnan, Farnsworth's Hardware Store, next Brett's Clothing Store. On far right was the Adams & Bayly Hardware Store. Kinnan, Farnsworth sign is in error. (Courtesy of San Juan County Historical Society)

Fig. 16. **Now**-Grand Imperial Hotel –August, 1998 (Allan G. Bird photo)

Fig. 17. **Then**-1884 photo showing the Congregational church, dedicated July 10, 1881, however, it was used in October, 1880. Note the old bell tower. The steeple was not built until 1892. (San Juan Co. Historical Society photo)

Fig. 18. **Now**-The United Church of Christ occupies the old 1880-81 Congregational church. (Allan Bird photo)

Page 18

2 p.m. (Fig 17). This building survives today and houses the United Church of Christ congregation. F. O. Sherwood built the original bell tower (not the present steeple) in early October, 1880. The children of the Sunday school purchased the bell. The entire cost of the tower and bell was $185. The steeple was added in June, 1892. The new church building held its first concert on October 2, 1880.

Two weeks before the completion of the church, a man by the name of McLaughlin came to the construction site to collect $10 owed him by a gent named

Claysen. Claysen and his young son were helping unload construction supplies from a wagon when McLaughlin approached demanding his money. Claysen ignored the demand, and McLaughlin pulled a gun, shooting Claysen in the neck.

Claysen collapsed in the wagon, falling on his small son. The doctors were able to save him. McLaughlin was sent to the Colorado State Penitentiary at Canon City.

On September 5, 1880, Silverton opened its first brewery (located at the southern end of Greene Street, at the foot of the mountain where the present highway to Durango begins its upward ascent). Mullholand & Peckham owned the brewery. Mullholand was one of the original 1871 pioneers. On February 4, 1881, the new brewery burned to the ground. The men of the town "by great exertion rescued the beer in the cellar." Several years later, Charles Fischer built a new stone building to house his brewery and ice plant (Fig. 19).

Fig. 19. **Then**-1907 photo of the Fischer Brewery. Located on the far south end of Greene Street where highway begins its ascent to Durango. (Eddie Lorenzon photo)

By 1881, all of the lots between 13th and 14th Streets were occupied by business houses and saloons. This was the central business district of Silverton (Fig. 12). The block to the south still contained a few empty lots.

A year earlier, on April 14, 1880, George Bayly & Company purchased the original Post Office Drug Store from C. S. & N.. On September 15, 1881, Bayly moved across the street into a new building recently completed for use as a post office (Fig. 20), next to Luesley's old stand, occupied by Asa Middaugh's General Store. The firm of Herr, Hodges, and Herr, who had just completed the Exchange Livery building a block to the south, moved into the old post office building and established a flour, feed, forwarding, and commission store. Contemporaneous with the construction of the new post office, Andrews and Anderson built a similar building next door to the south, to house their Crystal Palace Saloon (Fig. 20). Both buildings were joined by a common false front.

Fig. 20. **Then**-Geo. Bayly's Post Office Drug Store on right, Crystal Palace Saloon adjoining to the south. Saloon is 10 ft. narrower than post office. The building on far left encroached onto the lot where saloon stands. Wyman Hotel occupies post office site. Saloon site is now a vacant lot. (Ruth Gregory photo)

In May 1881, George Sitterly and Phil Friter built the Tiger Club Rooms (Fig. 12) on the vacant lot between the old C. S. & N. store and the old San Juan Bakery (now occupied by John and Isaac Montgomery). They installed two of Brunswick's latest improved billiard tables. Down the street, next door to the south of the Grand Central Hotel, Mart Stockman opened up a barber shop and news depot.

On June 10, Silverton experienced its second serious fire. The old 1874 store building of Greene & Eberhart (on upper Reese Street), burned to the ground. William Greene sold the building only days before to T. E. Bowman, who was using it to store hay. Some small boys playing with matches were believed to be the cause of the fire.

A block to the south stands Silverton's oldest business building, (Figs. 21 & 22) next door to the south of the large brick Posey & Wingate building on the corner. It was built in 1876 and occupied by Joseph Lacombe's General Store until

1879. The Posey & Wingate Hardware Company purchased the store and occupied it while they built their large two-story brick building next door. In 1881, a gentleman by the name of Emil Weinberger opened a wholesale liquor establishment and bar in the building. The Silverton bar owners had established a trade policy by which the price of hard liquor was set at 25 cents per shot. Weinberger came to town and promptly decided to cut the price to two-for-a-quarter. Weinberger came to work one July morning and found his store windows smashed. He immediately published a letter in the July 21, 1881, *San Juan Herald* which read:

An open letter to the supposed Saloon Keeper's Association: On Sunday morning I found a notice at my place of business, also my windows smashed in, notifying me that I must comply with their orders or suffer the consequences; and in a body resolved not to allow me to run their business. I do not propose to run anybody's business but my own. I pay all the law requires of me, and shall run it to suit myself and will sell my goods for any price I please, consequences or no consequences. According to the notice, I have every reason to believe that the Saloon Keepers smashed my windows or had something to do with it.

Emil Weinberger

A few days later, on July 28, unknown parties entered the store and destroyed his entire stock of wines, liquors, and cigars, causing $3,000 damage. This forced Weinberger to put his store up for sale. On August 18th, M. K. Cohen purchased the business and continued to sell drinks at two-for-a-quarter. By this time, the other saloonkeepers had given up and were beginning to lower their prices. Cohen was an interesting individual. He could be classed as a born loser. As our story of Silverton unfolds, we will hear more about M. K. Cohen.

Several blocks to the south, one of Silverton's great dramas was about to unfold. On May 9, 1881, Silverton's marshal, D. C. "Clate" Ogsbury arrived in town to take over his new position. Ogsbury was no stranger to the San Juans. He and his partner, J. H. Brink, had worked a claim near Howardsville in May, 1879. Ogsbury rented a small room in the rear of Johnny Goode's Senate Saloon (on the southeast corner of 13th and Greene Streets).

The Haley Brothers rented the old Diamond Saloon building (Fig. 24). The winter snows had caved in the roof. By the end of May, 1881, the Haley's had the building repaired and ready for business. The Diamond Saloon was actually a combination saloon, dance hall, and brothel. Its location on the far south end of town placed it out of the way of everyday life. The Haley's renamed the establishment the "Miner's Home." They planned to open a combination saloon, dance hall, and Variety Theater. The grand opening of the new theater was on June 25th, with the entertainment being, according to the *San Juan Herald*:

A very creditable affair. The banjo, violin, and tambourine players showed themselves to be experts, while the end men kept the audience in

Fig. 21. **Then**-1876 building built by Joseph Lacombe as a general store. The Silverton Standard newspaper occupied the building from 1952 to Sept. 30, 1998. The building now caters to the tourist trade. The 1880 Posey & Wingate brick building is to the right. (Colorado Historical Society photo)

Fig. 22. **Now**-May, 1999 photo of Joseph Lacombe's 1876 building. This is the oldest business building still standing. (Allan G. Bird photo)

Fig. 23. **Then**-1881 engraving of Silverton, Colorado. (Del Norte, Colorado, 1883 *San Juan Prospector*)

Fig. 24. **Then**-1883 photo showing the back of the Diamond Saloon building (arrow). The Congregational church is to the left. (Colorado Historical Society photo)

a roar of laughter by their jokes and witticisms.

A week later the paper stated:

> The variety entertainment of Haley Brothers and Maguire, referred to in our last issue has collapsed in thin air. The banjo and tambourine men have folded their tents, like the Arabs, and silently walked away. The people of Silverton evidently did not appreciate the talents of the 'star' actors; or else they were not altogether up to the secrets of the wine room-Quien Sabe.

The owners soon found that there was more profit in sin than variety entertainment. The next mention of the establishment, again referred to as the Diamond Saloon, was on August 24, 1881. A row occurred in the saloon when a miner from Ophir, by the name of Jack Lawsha, came over to imbibe and while away a few happy days. He was enticed by "Broncho Lou," the proprietress of the saloon, to enter her place of business. It was the first saloon on the road into Silverton. While there, he had a few glasses of wine and in doing so, exposed a couple one hundred dollar bills, two fifties and some smaller bills. When he came to, he had been rolled for $330. The marshal arrested "Lou" and placed her in jail. She was bound over for district court in the sum of $600. The paper summed it up with the biblical quote: "The way of the transgressor is hard." No mention of "Lou's" trial was made in subsequent issues because of the shocking event that happened a few days later. (Lou had a hand-full of husbands that all ended up dead)

On August 24, 1881, three members of the Stockton-Eskridge gang, rustlers and holdup men from Durango, arrived in Silverton. Bert Wilkinson, Dyson Eskridge, and a black man, known as "Kid" Thomas or the "Copper-Colored Kid," were seen drinking in the Diamond Saloon. Sheriff Thorniley and Marshal David Clayton Ogsbury were aware of their presence but having no warrant from La Plata County, decided to wait until the next day to make any arrests. About 11 o'clock on the evening of August 24, La Plata County Sheriff, Luke Hunter, arrived in town. He went to Goode's Saloon and awoke Ogsbury. Ogsbury suggested that they get help if an arrest was to be made that evening. Hunter convinced him that help was not necessary. Both men walked south down Greene Street. As Ogsbury approached the front of the Diamond Saloon, he saw a man in the shadows. He leaned forward to see who it was. Before he could say a word or reach for his gun, Burt Wilkinson and others started firing. Ogsbury was hit and killed almost instantly. The other men with Ogsbury ran for cover. The three desperados had left their horses at the Silverton Stable, about half-a-block north of the saloon. A group of men quickly rallied around Ogsbury and were carrying his body back to his room in the Senate Saloon. Wilkinson, Eskridge and the "Kid" could not reach their horses because these men were between them and the stable. The three took off on foot trying to get out of town. After about an hour they sent the "Copper-Colored Kid" back for the horses. For some reason, he went beyond the stables and was captured at the rear of the Grand Central Hotel and jailed. Search teams combed the hills for the remainder of the night to no avail. The following night, a mob broke into the old log jail and dragged the "Kid" to a shed at the rear of the county building, next door to Sherwin & Houghton's new stone store, now the Pickle Barrel Restaurant. They threw a rope around his neck and lynched him. There was no evidence that he actually took part in the shootings.

One of the mysteries of the whole event was the whereabouts of La Plata County Sheriff, Luke Hunter, during the melee. It appears that after the first shot, he turned an ran from the scene, abandoning his companions.

After a day or two of hard walking, Wilkinson and Eskridge made it to the Castle Rock Stage Station, about twenty miles north of Durango, where they were hidden and fed by Wilkinson's sister and her husband, Flora and Orville Pyle. Both men went into the woods with their fresh supplies and blankets and hid in a sparsely-traveled area. Only the Pyles knew where they were.

Word of the $2500 reward being offered by San Juan County and the merchants of Silverton reached their partner and gang leader, Ike Stockton, in Durango. Stockton decided to double-cross his friends for the reward money. He contacted Luke Hunter, who having been disgraced by his cowardly actions in Silverton was not anxious to go after the heavily armed men. He talked Hunter into deputizing himself and Bud Gilbreth, alias M. C. Cook. Both men had outstanding warrants for their arrest in other states. Stockton and Gilbreth arrived at the stage station and convinced Wilkinson's sister that they were there to help her brother and Eskridge escape. She accepted their story and told them where the two were hiding. Stockton and Gilbreth found their camp and told Dyson Eskridge, the larger of the two, to go to a ranch on the Pine River for fresh horses. He also chose Eskridge because he knew Dyson's brother, Harg, would kill him if he found out he had turned in his brother to Silverton authorities. After Eskridge had left, the two drew their guns on Bert Wilkinson and told him they were turning him in for the reward.

They took Wilkinson to a stone barn near Animas City (North Durango) and tied him securely. After several days of negotiations with Hunter and San Juan County authorities, Wilkinson was moved to a hotel. He was later moved back into the woods for fear that the Animas City and Durango citizens would lynch him if his presence became known. Arrangements were made with the officials at Silverton for Wilkinson's safe delivery. Stockton demanded assurances that he would not be harmed in Silverton, as there were outstanding warrants for his arrest. The sheriff gave him his personal assurance that he would be paid the reward money and escorted safely out of town.

Sheriff Thornily made arrangements with the La Plata County officials to escort the two to the San Juan County line, where he and a posse of twelve men would meet them. Wilkinson was locked up in the Silverton jail under heavy guard. Stockton was paid off and spent the night in the Walker House. In the morning, true to his word, Thorniley escorted Stockton to the edge of town with part of the reward money. The $2500 reward was for the capture of both men. It is believed that Stockton only received about $1400.

Wilkinson, who was only 19 years old, was well aware of his pending fate. His sister and brother-in-law arrived in Silverton Sunday morning and pleaded for a fair trial.

Sunday evening, a mob of vigilantes broke into the jail and told Wilkinson that his time was up. Wilkinson assisted them by climbing upon the chair and helping them place the rope around his neck. Asked if he had anything to say before the chair was pulled, he replied, "Nothing gentlemen, adios!" His only wish was to be left alone with Stockton for a few short minutes so they would have reason to hang him. This wish was never granted.

Sheriff Luke Hunter resigned his position in early September, 1881. He hoped that Stockton would be appointed to replace him but the city fathers chose a man by the name of Barry Watson. Watson did not trust the two ex-deputies living in a place where he was responsible for the peace and welfare of Animas City and Durango. He appointed Jim Sullivan, who had been Durango's first marshal, to go after both Stockton and Gilbreth. In late September, Stockton and Gilbreth rode their wagon from Animas City to Durango and pulled up in front of a building still under construction. Stockton went in the building and Watson and Sullivan arrested Gilbreth without incidence. They turned him over to another man for delivery to the jail. A short while later, Stockton came out of the building. Seeing the two lawmen, he ducked back into the doorway and drew his gun. Before he could get a shot off, both Watson and Sullivan fired almost simultaneously, hitting Stockton in the leg, just below the hip. The bullet shattered his femur and severed an artery. One newspaper account reported that he was taken to the San Juan Smelter office and allowed to bleed to death as no one would go for a doctor. Allan Nossaman, in his 1998 Vol. 3 edition of *Many More Mountains*, found a source that said no less than seven doctors arrived at the scene. They moved him to the new smelter office. They decided that the leg would have to be amputated if he were to have any chance of living. They amputated the leg at the point of the break but it was too late. Ike Stockton died at 2:45 the morning of September 26, 1881. He left a wife and two small children. He was only 29 years old. His body lies buried in the old Animas City Cemetery in Durango.

The Diamond Saloon was permanently closed after the incident. The saloon was located on the northeast corner of 11th and Greene Streets, between 25 and 50 feet from the corner facing Greene Street. This property is now a vacant lot next to the Lunch Box Restaurant. The saloon must have been a real shack (Fig. 24) as it was assessed for taxes at only $250. The vacant lot next door was assessed at $150.

+ CHAPTER 2 +

SILVERTON-THEN AND NOW   1882-1901

The *San Juan Herald* stated on January 5, 1882, "the town consisted of about 400 buildings and some 75 business houses, two hotels, and a fine church costing $5000 to build." A week later they said, "There are about 300 substantial, handsome and well-built dwellings and 50 business houses, including county and town public buildings." At any rate, "old" Silverton had a steady, but not rapid growth between 1875 and 1881.

1882 marked the beginning of a period of explosive growth brought on by the arrival of the Denver & Rio Grande Railroad, which reached Silverton on July 13, 1882. Several factors accounted for the relatively slow growth of the town: one, the lack of transportation, two, the lack of a bank. Until 1880, all money for payrolls and supplies had to come from the outside. Another restrictive factor was the severe winters. Around November 1, the majority of the merchant's closed shop and left for warmer climates, returning in early may. The deep snows made access to the mines almost impossible. Several mines operated during the winter. The men remained at the mines, depriving the merchants of badly needed business. This probably accounted for the rapid turnover of businesses. It was not uncommon to have a building occupied by two or more tenants during the time frame of one year.

The arrival of the railroad brought favorable changes in mining economics. Lower grade ores could be mined at a profit. The railroad brought an influx of money and people to Silverton that bolstered the shaky wintertime businesses. The introduction of the aerial tramway, a ski tow-type device with buckets for carrying ore attached, brought ores and men from the high-country mines to lower altitudes. This assured a steady flow of customers and money during the winter months.

During the spring of 1882, several new buildings were begun. The excavation for the Thomson Block (Grand Imperial Hotel) began in May. By July, 1882, there were two brick making firms in Silverton. The foundations and bricks for the new Thomson building were made from locally produced bricks. The building was a monumental undertaking for Silverton. It was to be 100 feet along the front and 75 feet deep, having four stores on the main floor, offices and town council rooms on the second floor, and hotel rooms on the third. Mr. W. S. Thomson was from London, England. His partner, Dr. S. H. Beckworth, was in charge of building the new Martha Rose Smelter near the south edge of town. The hotel and smelter were

Fig. 25. **Then**-1885 photo. Looking north from 12ᵗʰ Street. The Grand Hotel is on the left. Jane Bowen's Westminster Hall Saloon and Bordello is on the far right. Only one building remains on the right side of the street. It is now occupied by the Pickle Barrel Restaurant. (Ruth Gregory photo)

Fig. 26. **Then**-1892 photo of the Grand Hotel. The sign on the awning reads Post Office. (Eddie Lorenzon photo)

of a joint project.

At the time of construction, Silverton was a wild place. The August 10, 1882, edition of the *San Juan Herald* reported:

> Pistol firing has been too promiscuous on some portions of lower Greene Street of late. No one likes to have a bullet whistling past their ears in broad daylight, or any other time for that matter, even if the 'shooters' do it just for fun. The village authorities should put a check reign on this thing.

The same edition of the paper mentioned that the dirt and gravel from the Thomson building excavation was being used to grade the streets of Silverton.

By late October, the exterior of the building was undergoing its final touches. The October 26, 1882, *San Juan Herald* wrote:

> The iron front for the Thomson's new block arrived the first of the week and has been put in place and the brickwork is now progressing at a rapid rate. The walls are complete with the exception of the front, and the frame work for the mansard roof is all done and ready to be put in place, which will be done the first of next week. Mr. Melville says that if the weather will keep nice until next Wednesday all the outdoor work will be completed and the building enclosed.

The grand opening of the new building was scheduled for April 1, 1883. All that remained was to install the large 64 X 84-inch French plate glass windows on the front of the building. On the third week of March, the box of windows arrived. Upon opening the crates, they found the glass smashed into a thousand pieces. The railroad refused to cover the costs and the owners had to absorb the $1113 loss. The windows were reordered. The April 19 paper announced that the Thomson block was completed. It is difficult to comprehend how a building of that size could be completed in less than a year when one considers that all the excavation and carpentry work was done by hand without the use of power equipment.

The four main floor tenants promptly moved in. On April 17, 1883, Brett & Company, a men's clothing store, moved into what is now the hotel lobby. Ira Kruschke's Silverton Bazaar, a Durango clothing company, rented the corner store. Next door, where the bar and dining room now stand, the hardware business of Kinnan, Farnsworth & Company established quarters. Adams & Bayly of Durango, another hardware store, occupied the last store on the north end of the building. The four new tenants consisted of two clothing stores and two hardware stores, each 25 feet wide and 75 feet deep. A ten-foot American flag was placed on the roof of the building.

Changes were made on the others floors of the building. The county leased most of the second floor for county offices and courtrooms. The hotel on the third floor wasn't opened for business until May 10, 1883, "to be run on the European Plan." It was to have 40 rooms. This number is probably a gross exaggeration as the present hotel has only 23 rooms on the third floor. There were no baths in the original hotel rooms. If you subtracted the baths from the present rooms, each room would have to be about the size of a small jail cell to accommodate 40 rooms.

When the owners finally made the third floor into a hotel, they took much of the back space of the Adams & Bayly Hardware store and made it into a large dining room, capable of seating all of the residents of the hotel. It is questionable if Adam's & Bayly survived more than a short period, as the space in front of the dining room occupied by their store became the hotel lobby.

When the Thomson group decided to build the hotel building, Tom Blair sold his two vacant lots for $1. There must have been some other financial arrangements with Thomson as Blair moved his Rose Bud Saloon to the back of the lot and built the "Assembly Rooms," a saloon and gambling establishment, in front of his old building (Fig. 28). The paper reported, "The architecture being put on the front of Tom Blair's new saloon is certainly very too, too, for this town, but it looks very nice for all that and excites much comment." It was actually a one-and-a-half story false-front with a triangle-shaped motif above the upper story window. This was the third building to be constructed on this lot. The original building was Bush's Blacksmith Shop. Blair tore this structure down and built his Rose Bud Saloon.

Fig. 27 shows the main business district in the late summer of 1881. This photo is dated by the lack of a sign on the county building, second from the right (Where "Kid Thomas" was lynched about the time this photo was taken). The county moved out about mid-July and took their sign with them. Robert Ambold moved his Silverton Meat Market into the building in November, 1881.

Two doors beyond the Olympic Saloon is the sign of Fleming the druggist (Fig. 29). Lazarus & Rapp's Clothing Store originally occupied this building. Lazarus and Rapp had moved into a temporary building while their new store was being built in the summer of 1880. Fleming moved in on June 1, 1881, and remained until March, 1887. This is one of the oldest surviving buildings on Greene Street.

Silverton had a fire bell tower in the middle of 13th Street, a few feet west of Greene Street. The original tower was torn down in May, 1882. The new tower had a bandstand built around it, which is visible in the 1883 photo (Fig. 31).

On March 1, 1882, Ed Gorman and Kaltenback purchased the Tivoli Saloon. This was the old Brown & Cort Saloon (Fig. 27).

In May, George Pile & Company opened a dry goods store in the old county building, (Fig. 27) recently occupied by Ambold Brother's Meat Market. In August, the operator of the firm, Mr. Head, had been troubled with someone lurking around his home at night. He took up watch and was rewarded by the arrival of the midnight "lurker." He fired two shots at the villain, one of which hit the intruder in the loins (wherever the loins are). The man proved to be a black man who was working for the Martha Rose Smelter. The *San Juan Herald*, in its usual merciful outlook, wrote:

> He has at least been taught one important lesson and if these house sneaks, whether colored or white, were occasionally treated to a dose of cold lead, it might teach them to follow a more honorable and profitable

Fig. 27. **Then**-1881 view of Greene Street north of 13th Street. Building on the far left is Tom Blair's Rose Bud Saloon. This building was demolished to make room for Tom Blair's Assembly Rooms Saloon and Gambling Hall. (Colorado Historical Society photo)

Fig. 28. **Then**-West side of Greene Street looking southwest from 14th Street. Tom Blair's Assembly Rooms Saloon occupied the one-and-a-half-story building in the center in 1883. The photo taken in 1894 when the Assembly Rooms building was occupied by Kramer's Meat Market. (Ruth Gregory photo)

Fig. 29. **Then**-Fleming's Drug Store. Fleming occupied the store from 1881 to 1887. It was built in the summer of 1880. (Den. Pub. Lib. West. Hist. Dept. photo)

Fig. 30. **Now**-Old Fleming Drug Store building. August, 1998. (Allan G. Bird photo)

Fig. 31. **Then**-July 4, 1883 photo of the west side of Greene Street looking south from 14th Street. Tom Blair's Assembly Rooms Saloon is on the far left. The Arlington Saloon, formerly Tom White's Olympic Saloon, is second from the left. (Ruth Gregory photo)

Fig. 32. **Now**-August, 1998 photo showing the same view as Fig. 31. (Allan G. Bird photo)

pastime than sneaking around private residences. Mr. Head ought to have the thanks of the town for teaching one vagabond, at least, a wholesome lesson.

On May 23, Tom Cain, a crooked lawman, sold the Odeon Dance Hall to his brother, Pat, for $2500. The Odeon was located on the east side of Greene Street, three doors south of 12th Street. This was one of Silverton's oldest bordellos. The bill of sale listed: bar equipment and liquors, eight beds, eight wash basins, and eight mirrors. Not your everyday saloon equipment.

Silverton's jail facilities were less than satisfactory. The old town log jail, where Bert Wilkinson was lynched, was contracted to Jesse Love for $550. He completed the jail in August, 1875. The jail was located on the west side of Blair Street, north of 13th street, behind what was then a structure used as the county building. The jail, for some unknown reason, was built diagonally on the lot. This jail was compared to a pigsty by the town council (Figs. 35 & 36).

The county built a new stone jail, which was completed in late November, 1882. The structure still stands, in the alley between Blair and Mineral Streets, north of 13th Street. Another building now covers the front of the jail. The rear is plainly visible in the alley (Fig. 38).

For years the location of the old log jail was unknown. In January, 1985, a fire developed in a small frame house. The fire revealed that the old log jail had been aligned with the lot lines and covered with siding to become part of a private residence. The log and barred window of the jail (Fig. 35) are now on display in the San Juan County Historical Society Museum next to the courthouse.

In 1883, the town built a new wooden plank jail behind the city hall on Blair Street (Fig. 37). This structure has been moved several times in past years and today stands on the southeast corner of 13th and Blair Streets. It serves as a gift shop.

In 1902, the county built a substantial brick jail next to the present courthouse (Figs.40 & 41). The structure now houses the San Juan County Historical Society Museum. The prisoners were kept in steel cells upstairs while the sheriff and his family lived on the main floor. The sheriff's wife usually cooked the meals for the prisoners.

Corky Scheer, one of Silverton's colorful old-timers (Fig. 34), was the last person to escape from this jail. He was a small-framed man and had been arrested for drunk driving down the sidewalk in front of the Imperial Hotel. It was wintertime and the snow was banked against the curb. He decided to race down the sidewalk between the buildings and the snow bank. The town sheriff and marshal were drinking coffee in the Imperial Hotel when he roared past their window. He was sentenced to 30 days. He had a girlfriend who lived in the brick house to the east of the jail. He would signal her with a mirror and drop a long piece of string out the window. She would tie a bottle of whiskey to the string. He kept himself drunk during most of his sentence. He complained how cold it was, as the jail had no central heating system. St. Patrick's day was approaching and Corky wanted to go to the local dance being held in the Miner's Union Hall, now the American Legion building. On the night of the dance, Corky waited until the sheriff left the jail to make his rounds. He took off all his clothes and threw them out the small iron window (Fig. 33) that was used to pass food to the prisoners. Two of the bars had been sawed off for access of the dinner plates. He wiggled and twisted through the small opening, finally making his way out. The small iron stubs left where they cut off the two bars left him cut and bleeding but he was out and on his way to the dance.

When the sheriff returned from his rounds, he found Corky missing and knew immediately where he had gone. As the sheriff entered the front door of the dance hall, Corky saw him and headed out the back door. They played hide and seek for most of the evening. The sheriff knew that Corky's girl friend lived across the street. He figured that would be where he would be hiding. He knocked on her door, knowing she would not reveal his presence. He told her to tell Corky that the cell was open and he expected him to be in it in the morning. When morning came, Corky was sound asleep in his cell. Corky passed away in the early 1990's.

The last town jail was completed in 1910 in the new town hall (Fig 39).

Fig. 33. **Now**-Jail window from which Corky Scheer escaped from the county jail in the 1930's. Now the San Juan County Historical Society Museum. (Allan G. Bird photo-1998)

Fig. 34. **Recent**-1986 photo of Corky Scheer in front of the 1902 jail from which he escaped. Now a museum. (Allan G. Bird photo)

Fig. 35. **Now**-Bars from the 1875 log jail where Bert Wilkinson was lynched. Now on display in the San Juan County Historical Society 1902 jail museum. (Allan G. Bird photo)

Fig. 36. **Now**-Site of 1875 log jail. Silverton's first jail. Located on the west side of Blair Street between 13th and 14th Streets. (Allan G. Bird photo)

Fig. 37. **Now**-1883 wooden plank jail. Originally located behind the 1883 town hall on Blair Street. Now on the southeast corner of 13th and Blair Streets. Used until 1910. (Allan G. Bird-May, 1999 photo)

Fig. 38. **Now**-1882 stone county jail. Located in the alley between Blair and Mineral Streets, north of 13th Street. (Allan G. Bird photo)

Fig. 39. **Now**-Last jail in Silverton.. Completed in July, 1910. The town jail is on the right side of the main floor. Not used for years. All prisoners are now taken to Durango. (Allan G. Bird photo)

Fig. 40. **Then**-1902 county jail. Photo taken c.a. 1920. South entrance. (Mrs. Geo. VanBoken photo)

Fig. 41. **Now**-1989 photo of the 1902 county jail. Now the San Juan County Historical Society Museum. (Allan G. Bird photo)

On March 24, 1883, Mr. George Brower of Denver, rented Tom White's Olympic Saloon and Dining Hall. He completely refurbished the building into a deluxe saloon and gambling hall, naming it the Arlington (Fig. 40). Brower had his grand opening on April 21. Durango pianist Professor Cariner and Denver violinist Mr. Kettie, provided the music. The back-bar was of black walnut with finely-carved French veneer work along with one of the finest mirrors in Silverton.

Brower hired a rather famous individual, by the name of Wyatt Earp, to run his gambling rooms. This was two years after Earp had his showdown at the O. K. Corral in Tombstone, Arizona Territory. Some said that Earp had come to Silverton to escape an outstanding murder warrant. This is only speculation. In early May, the Denver papers wrote that Wyatt Earp was a member of the gang that was on their way to Dodge City, Kansas to forcefully re-enter the town.

Luke Short, one of Wyatt's friends, also a gambler, was in partnership with Harris and Beeson. They owned the Long Branch Saloon in Dodge City, one of the largest and best gambling houses in Dodge. The Dodge City mayor, a man named Webster, also ran a gambling house next door to Luke Short's. As Short was from Texas, he attracted a large number of Texans who were herding cattle to Dodge City from Texas. Webster decided to put Luke out of business and passed an ordinance banning music in saloons and gambling houses. Luke agreed to this as he saw it as a way to cut expenses. The first night after the ordinance went into effect, Luke noticed that music was coming from Webster's place next door. The next night, he hired his musicians back and waited to see what would happen. As all was quiet, he decided to take a short trip to visit a sick friend. When he returned, he found that all of his musicians, including a woman piano player, had been arrested and put in jail. Luke tried to find someone to bail them out but all of the elected officials suddenly vanished from sight. While Luke was trying to bail out his band, loud music was coming from the bar next door. It was late at night and Luke had given up trying to bail out his crew when he encountered the officer that had arrested them. Without warning, the officer drew his gun and fired, missing Short. Short returned the fire. The officer fell to the ground to avoid the bullets but was not hit. Short saw him go down and figured he had hit him. He went back to his saloon and got his shotgun. He spent the rest of the night defending himself from the Mayor's men. The next morning a truce was called. If Luke would agree to pay a small fine and plead guilty to disturbing the peace, they would drop the whole affair. Luke turned in his gun but was immediately arrested and taken to jail. Two trains a day passed through Dodge City, one going east, the other west. Both trains arrived at noon. Short was taken to the train station and given a choice of which direction he wanted to go. He knew he would be shot if he stayed. He took the eastern train to Kansas City.

Once in Kansas City, he wired W. B. "Bat" Masterson to come to Kansas City, which he did. Both Luke Short and Masterson traveled to Topeka, the capital of Kansas and met with the governor. They told him their story but the governor refused to intervene in the matter. He did, however, give his assurance that if Short and his friends did go back and try to forcefully re-enter Dodge, he would keep the state officials out of the fight.

Bat Masterson boarded a train for Denver and Silverton to try and enlist the help of Wyatt Earp. Luke Short went to Caldwell, Kansas, where he had a couple of friends he knew would join the fight.

Earp readily agreed to leave Silverton and help his friends. The May 12, 1883, *Silverton Democrat* wrote:

> The Club Rooms of the Arlington are conducted by Wyatt Earp who is a pleasant and affable gentleman, and not mixed up in the Dodge City broils, as the Denver papers would have us believe, and the editorial paragraph in the *Denver Republican* of the 16th (How could they quote the 16th on the 12th?) placing him at the scene of action and counseling the citizens of Dodge to take the law in their own hands, is wholly unwarranted, from the fact that Mr. Earp is now, and has for the past three months, been a peaceable and law-abiding citizen of Silverton, and not been in Dodge City for the last four years.

It was true that up until the above article was written, Earp had been working in Silverton. A few days after the article, Brower decided to remodel the Arlington and added one of the largest bar mirrors in the state, being 18 feet long. He also added a street lamp in front of the saloon, which is visible in Fig. 42. It was during this time that Masterson probably arrived in Silverton. Wyatt Earp left Silverton with Masterson and never returned.

When Earp and Masterson arrived in Kansas, a small army of some of the West's roughest characters had assembled to help Luke Short. The roster read like a page from a Western novel: "Rowdy Joe", Doc Holiday, Charles Bassett, Shotgun Collins (well known in Silverton), Jim Calhoun, Wyatt Earp and Bat Masterson.

When word of their impending arrival reached Dodge, Mayor Webster called a hasty meeting of his friends. None of the group had anticipated having to take part in a gunfight in which they were sure to lose. They sent a message to Earp and asked him to come to Dodge and act as a mediator. Earp accepted the invitation and told Webster that unless the music ordinance was repealed and Luke Short was allowed to return and conduct his business as usual, their blood would flow in the streets of Dodge. Webster and his gang quickly retreated and all of Earp's demands were met. Earp assured them that if they kept their word there would be no bloodshed.

Luke Short and Bat Masterson arrived on the noon train, Short had won. Webster never gave him any more trouble.

The short visit of Bat Masterson to Silverton probably gave birth to the myth that Masterson was hired by Silverton city fathers to clean up Silverton's gambling and prostitution. The fact of the matter was that the city fathers did not want the town cleaned up. The saloons and prostitutes provided their primary source of revenue and eliminated the need for city property taxes. Masterson never worked in Silverton.

Fig. 42 was taken on July 4, 1883. It shows the fire bell and gazebo located in the street in front of the Arlington Saloon. The photo was taken from the northeast corner of 14th and Greene Streets looking south. Herr, Hodges & Herr's store along with John Montgomery's sign date the photo as 1883.

Fig. 42. **Then**-1883 photo showing the Arlington Saloon, 2nd from the right. Looking south from the northeast corner of 14th and Greene Streets. (Ruth Gregory photo)

Fig. 43. **Now**-The left half of the building was the site of the Arlington Saloon where Wyatt Earp worked. The above Cole-Hoffman building was built in 1902. (Allan G. Bird photo-August, 1998)

Fig. 44 shows the Matthews and Walton store across the street from the Silverton Hotel. This is the original 1875 Luesley store, later Asa Middaugh's Grocery Store and Charles Bayles' Furniture Store. Matthews and Walton opened on August 8, 1881. On June 2, 1883, Matthews sold out to Walton. Walton painted a small for sale sign on the building after Matthews left.

H. P. Walton became innovative in July, 1883. He purchased a "high-up daisy, double-spring delivery wagon." The paper stated, "he was a rusher for sure." Home deliveries must have been the "out thing" in those days. A week after Walton put his delivery wagon on the road, some unhappy competitor thew a stick of dynamite under his horse. Walton offered a $100 reward, "for the conviction of the villainous person or persons who threw giant powder in my stable and under my horse----H. P. Walton, July 20, 1883." No mention was made of what happened to the horse, but we can guess.

Fig. 44. **Then**-1881 photo showing Matthews & Walton's store. The building with the large sign on the side, across the street from the Silverton Hotel. Trees were cut and placed in front of the stores for decoration. The Wyman Hotel now stands on the site of Matthews & Walton's store. (Den. Pub. Library Western History Dept. photo)

In May, 1883, McMillian and Marshal reopened Pat Cain's old Odeon Dance Hall as a new variety theater. The building had been enlarged and improved, with six double boxes added making it convenient for "dandies and daisies on the side." A month after the opening, Mr. McMillian was tried and convicted of swindling a widow with five children out of her life savings. McMillian had worked for the woman's husband. When the husband died, she was left with a herd of cattle. She hired McMillian to take the cattle to Denver and sell them. He sold them at a heavy loss. He then convinced her to take the $2400 and invest in theater. He invested $610 in the theater and squandered the rest, leaving her penniless. Judge Gerry sentenced McMillian to five years in the state penitentiary at Canon City. Judge Gerry was the same judge that later sentenced Alfred Packer, the Lake City cannibal, to hang.

On July 14, the Odeon Theater was closed and the furniture and fixtures sold. The building was reopened on August 9 as the Rose Bud Saloon (the name taken from Tom Blair's original saloon) by William Dennis. He died two years later of miner's consumption (silicosis) at the age of 34.

Fig. 45. **Then**-July 4, 1891 photo showing building formerly occupied by the Odeon Dance Hall, later the Odeon Theater, followed by the Rose Bud Saloon. Sign on building in 1891 reads Ten Pin Alley. Photo taken from just south of 12th Street looking north. The building is now gone. (San Juan Co. Hist. Society photo)

In 1883, the town fathers decided to build a new town hall on the west side of Blair Street between 12th and 13th Streets. The building was of frame construction, two-stories high, with the fire department occupying the ground floor and the town offices upstairs. Dances were frequently held on the second floor. When the decision was made to build on Blair Street, most of the gambling and prostitution

Fig. 46. **Then**-1914 photo showing the 1883 Town Hall on Blair Street. (Colo. Historical Society photo)

Fig. 47. **Now**-1883 Town Hall in August, 1998. The top floor has been removed and a new false front recently built. Located on the west side of Blair Street, between 12th and 13th Streets. (Allan G. Bird photo)

was located on Greene Street. In late 1884, the town fathers passed an ordinance limiting prostitution to and area encompassed by the alley between Greene and Blair Streets and 10th and 14th Streets. Thus Blair Street became the official Red Light District of Silverton, much to the consternation of the "proper" ladies of Silverton who needed to do business in the town hall. The January 9, 1886, *Silverton Democrat* wrote with disgust about the fusion of the two social elements in an article entitled:

Two Balls In One Night

We have seen 'ten nights in a bar room,' and ten bar rooms in a night: but last evening was the first opportunity we ever had to see two balls in the same room in one night. While we did not attend either, we are assured by parties who attended both that each was a grand success.

For the past week, the Reese Ball, to be given at the town hall Friday evening, January 8th, had been the talk of society circles in the city, and the turnout last evening was large and embraced the best and most highly respected element of Silverton society. The ball was in every feature a success, and, in harmony with a modest and temperate appreciation of the proprieties, the ball broke up at 1 a. m. The ladies were escorted to their moral and happy homes, and we regret to say, that in some cases their escorts returned to the ball to attend the second ball of the evening—for no sooner had the respectable element left the ball and it was taken possession of by the *demi-monde*—and to the strains of the same music and beneath the same lights, with a change of partners, began the Bacchanalian orgies of abandoned revelry. Beneath the careluie (sic) light, with flagrant suggestiveness, the racquet, the shadow, and the can-can were gone through to the finish.

It was between five and six o'clock this morning when ball number two ended.

The indignation of the respectable ladies of our city, who attended the first ball, is just. It is an insult to them, which deserves the indignant resentment of all good people. It will have a tendency to render fatal all efforts to get up a respectable social ball in the future. If it were intended for a joke, the parties who are responsible for it should be reminded that it is one which partakes of the character of an insult to every virtuous wife, mother, or sister in the city.

On June 2, 1883, the grand opening of the new Temple of Fashion Saloon and Variety Theater, attracted the attention of the entire town (Figs. 48 & 49). The building was a two-story false-front, located two doors south of the Exchange Livery. (The Outdoor World Sport Shop, Fig. 50, now stands on the lot). It was reported to be the finest in the southwest. In November, a new dining room was added to the establishment. It featured an elegant menu of duck, quail, prairie chicken, rabbit, turkey, and geese on order at all hours. Shell oysters were also offered. The September 8 paper stated, "A lady that used to sing before the crowned heads of Europe is now singing before the deadheads of Silverton at the Fashion Saloon." The reputation of the Fashion went downhill fast. By August, 1884 the Fashion was listed for sale. Mr. W. E. Ellis, one of the owners, took off for parts unknown with the cash box leaving the performers shy a week's wages and his partner, Mr. M. W. Williams, in a very awkward position. All of the assets were heavily mortgaged. The sheriff closed the operation on September 16, 1885. By December, the Fashion was reopened under new management. The *La Plata Miner* wrote in mid-December:

> A crowd of 'tin-horns' and prostitutes indulged in a wild drunken orgy at the Fashion on Tuesday night and were in full possession of the house for quite a while; they then adjourned to Harry LeRoy's place (The Metropolitan Saloon) and bedlam reigned supreme. Two of the women were arrested, and it is too bad the entire party were not lodged in the refrigerator.

Fig.48. **Then**-1905 photo showing the 1883 Temple of Fashion Saloon and Variety Theater building. (Fritz Klinke photo)

Fig. 49. **Then**-1883 sketch of the interior of the Temple of Fashion Saloon, Gambling Hall, and Variety Theater. Located on the east side of Greene Street between 12th and 13th Streets. (Sketch from the Nov. 23, 1883 edition of the *Silverton Democrat*)

Fig. 50. **Now**-Built in 1972, the Outdoor World building occupies the site of the long-since demolished Temple of Fashion Saloon. (Allan G. Bird, May, 1999 photo)

In August, 1883, Tom Cain, the saloon and dance hall owner, was appointed town marshal. Silverton's early law enforcement men were often chosen from the lower elements of society, i.e. saloon or brothel owners. It took extra tough men for the job and these men usually fit the job description.

On November 25, 1883, a shooting occurred between Marshal Cain and his neighbor and competitor, Riley Lambert. Cain's saloon was located on the southeast corner of 13th and Blair Streets where the old 1883 wooden plank jail now stands. Lambert had a saloon next door to the south. The *Silverton Democrat*, gave a detailed account of the shooting in the December 1, 1883, issue. The story read as follows:

Riley Lambert Shot

On Sunday morning last an affray occurred between Riley Lambert, proprietor of one of the dance halls here and Thomas Cain, city marshal, the result of which was to leave both parties wounded. Cain receiving a shot through the right cheek, which was a close call for the jugular vein, and Lambert being shot through the body. The ball entering just below the left nipple, passing diagonally across and under the right set of ribs, being extracted about five inches below the back of the right nipple. Drs. Lawrence and Murray have been in constant attendance on Lambert, but give no encouragement for his recovery as the course of the ball renders it almost a certainty the liver was wounded. The facts in regard to this affray as we gathered them from an eyewitness, are as follows: A number of parties who had been up all night in the dance hall, were in the morning making more of a disturbance than the night police deemed proper, and Harry LeRoy went to the hall for the purpose of quieting it. A good deal of loud and threatening talk was being made and LeRoy, thinking that trouble was brewing, left the hall and went to awaken Cain, who was at that time asleep. After doing this, he came on the street and saw a man from the dance hall named Leddy going into Posey, Wingate & Heffron's hardware store. Suspecting his errand he promptly followed him and found him buying cartridges. LeRoy arrested him and placed him in the calaboose. Just after doing this, Lambert came to the officer and endeavored to secure Leddy's release, which LeRoy could not grant, and while talking with Lambert, Marshal Cain came through the alleyway leading to the jail, and Lambert asked him to release Leddy. This Cain refused to do, saying that in the condition Leddy was in he might make trouble, but agreed to leave the question of his release to the mayor. This plan did not suit Lambert, and exclaiming, "If money won't get him out, this will," he pulled his pistol and shot Cain, the ball striking him in the face. Cain immediately closed with Lambert and seizing the pistol with his left hand, endeavored to wrest it from him. In the scuffle Lambert shot again, but without effect save the tearing of a large hole in Cain's coat and setting it on fire. By this time

Cain had pulled his pistol out and shot, the ball striking Lambert as before described. Lambert then broke from Cain who fired a second shot, but without effect. Lambert then dropped his pistol and staggering a few steps, sunk to the ground. LeRoy came to him and raising him up, asked him if he was badly hurt, and for a reply Lambert took his knife from his pocket and ripped his shirt down to see the wound himself. By this time other parties appeared on the scene and Lambert was assisted to his room. This account we believe to be substantially correct and fully justifies Marshal Cain by his action. The position he fills is not an enviable one, but he has been a faithful and efficient officer whose whole aim has been to preserve order, and enforce the law. In this he has been, and will be heartily sustained by our citizens, even though he be compelled to resort to the most extreme measures in the performance of his duties.

Later: Lambert died at 4:30 p. m. on Wednesday.

Riley Lambert had left an estate of $10,000 to his brothers. For years after the shooting, the feeling among many of the local people was that Cain shot first. The story reported by the witnesses, who were for the most part Cain's friends, was made up to cover the fact that there had been a long-standing feud between Cain and Lambert. Cain wanted Lambert dead. Shortly before the shooting, Tom's brother, Pat Cain, arrived in Silverton for a visit. By this time Pat had sold his Odeon Dance Hall and was the town marshal of Rico, Colorado. After the shooting, Tom Cain left for six weeks to visit his home in Wisconsin. There was speculation that he would not return.

The next that was heard of Tom Cain was a rather complimentary comment written by the *Silverton Democrat* on March 22, 1884. It read:

'Law and order' Bosh! Silverton had never been more orderly than it has in the past year. While we are not particularly 'stuck' on Tom Cain, we assert that Silverton has never had a better marshal. That he has not kept order cannot be said by his bitterest enemies.

The following spring Tom and Pat Cain's names came to the forefront again in Silverton. Pat Cain and Phillip Mahar had murdered Billy Wilson. Tom was deeply involved in the cover-up story and bribery of a local judge. On June 22, 1884, the *Silverton Democrat* reported the following story:

Last Sunday morning (June 22nd) the city was considerably excited over the information that a man had been killed near Silverton. The facts, as near as we can gather, were that Pat Cain, Phil Mahar, and Billy Wilson were out for a ride and started up the road to Red Mountain, and after getting near Burro Bridge, about six miles from town, the three got off to get a drink at a spring, when from some cause, firing commenced and Billy Wilson was killed. Cain and Mahar returned to Silverton and surrendered to the authorities. A coroner's jury was impaneled and immediately went to the scene of the affray and, after viewing the body, it was brought to town and the jury went into secret deliberation. After being in session until Monday evening, they brought in the following verdict: 'We find that said William Wilson came to his death on the 22d of June, A.D. 1884, about six miles from Silverton on the Ophir and San Miguel Toll Road, by gunshot wounds from pistols in the hands of Patrick Cain and Phillip Mahar, who did then and there willfully and feloniously kill and murder the said William Wilson within the County of San Juan and State of Colorado.'

The coroner issued a warrant for Cain and Mahar, in accordance with the verdict and they were placed in the county jail. On Tuesday they were arraigned before Justice Bryant and pled not guilty to the charge and were remanded to jail without bail.

The defendants claimed that the shooting of Wilson was in self-defense, but as the testimony was not clear on that part they were both held for premeditated murder. The preliminary examination was set for next Monday.

Wilson was a sporting character here and was well known throughout the county. He was 34 years of age and was a native of Wisconsin.

The funeral occurred last Tuesday, and was largely attended. The body was taken to the church where a few appropriate and impressive remarks were made by Rev. Bullock, after which the procession, led by a band playing a dirge, proceeded to the cemetery where the remains were laid to rest.

Evidenced surfaced to the effect that Tom Cain had bribed Judge Bryant to release Pat Cain and Phil Mahar on a light bail. The July 3, 1884, *San Juan Herald* came out and openly accused Bryant of taking a bribe, even though they could not show definite proof. The paper stirred up the citizens of Silverton and the following letter was the result:

Letter to C. M. Bryant from 'Many Citizens'

Your actions have been very closely watched since the preliminary examination of Cain and Mahar was placed in your hands and while we the citizens, intend that they shall have a trial by jury for the crime they are charged with instead of being lynched, as we don't consider that the man they murdered was any great loss to society, we intend also that the law shall have its course in the premises and as your conduct in the last few days has been somewhat suspicious in conversing with sworn witnesses of Cain and Mahar, and further while we don't wish to intimidate you in any way whatever and while, we have good reason to believe that advances have been made you by

Cain's friends we would advise you that it isn't policy for you to be partial towards them in any way whatever. (Signed 'Many Citizens')

It is interesting to note that the deciding factor that determined if a man was to be lynched or taken to trial, was his worth. When Bert Wilkinson killed Marshal Ogsbury in 1881, Wilkinson and the "Copper-Colored Kid" were lynched by a mob within days after their capture because Marshal Ogsbury was "loved by all." Billy Wilson was a saloon bum and pimp. Nobody gave a damn about his fate.

During the following week, the case went to trial. Numerous witnesses were called for both the prosecution and the defense. Sheriff William Sullivan testified that Pat and Tom Cain had come into his office to report that Pat and Phillip Mahar had shot Billy Wilson in self-defense and wanted to give themselves up. Pat Cain turned over two revolvers to Sullivan, a .38 and a .45-caliber. Pat told Sullivan that Mahar had nothing to do with the shooting. Sheriff Sullivan put both men in the city jail until an investigation of the killing could be made. The sheriff then mounted his horse and rode six miles to the scene of the crime, at Burro Bridge on the road to Red Mountain Town (The present Ouray road). He reached the body and found a local Silverton man, Tom Moss, sitting on the bank of the stream near the body. Tom handed Sullivan a .41-caliber pistol that he had found near the body, along with $172.35 plus some jewelry he had found on Wilson's body. Dr. Pascoe and Mike Larnagan were also present when Sullivan arrived.

Tom Moss was called to the stand and placed under oath. He testified that he had met Billy Wilson early that morning and Billy had asked him what he was doing up so early? Tom replied that "he was going out to hunt some lost horses." The next time Tom saw Billy, he was lying dead by the roadside near Burro Bridge. Moss said that he had found the .41-caliber pistol lying by Wilson's right hip and a handkerchief by his left hand. There was a large pool of blood in the road about 30 paces from where he had found the body. Tom Moss told the court that his first thought was that Wilson had committed suicide.

Dr. Pascoe testified that he was on his way to Chattanooga, a small community on the road to Red Mountain Town, when he found the body. Wilson was lying on his back and had apparently been moved from where he had died. Dr. Pascoe said that it looked to him that the pistol had been placed by his side.

Pat Cain was next called to the stand. Pat claimed that he and Phillip Mahar were planning a trip to Ophir and invited Billy to join them. He agreed and the three stopped off at Goode's Saloon for a drink and some cigars. Before leaving town they stopped at the new beer garden, which was located near the Martha Rose Smelter, for another drink. When they reached Burro Bridge, they dismounted to get a drink of water from a spring. Wilson said he saw a rabbit and asked Phil for his gun. Phil handed him his .41-caliber revolver and he immediately leveled the gun at Pat saying, "Cain, defend yourself," at the same time firing a shot. Billy missed and Cain drew both of his revolvers, a .41 and .45-caliber, and started firing. According to Cain, Wilson got off three shots before he was hit by Cain's fire. Cain swore that all three men were sober, even though they had stopped for a few drinks before leaving town.

Phillip Mahar was called next. He concurred with Pat Cain's testimony but said he had obtained his gun, a .41-caliber revolver, from Ed Gorman's bar early that morning. In later testimony, both Ed Welch, Gorman's bartender, and Ed Gorman denied that they had given Mahar a gun.

Wilson's girl friend, Nellie vanCamp, was called to the stand. She stated that she had been living with Billy for three years. She further testified that Billy had left his gun in the room that morning. Nellie was one of Blair Street's "working girls." Billy was her pimp.

The next witness was J. W. Heck. He told the court that he was coming from Ophir on his way to Silverton and had found a pool of blood a short distance from where the body lay. In the blood-soaked ground he had found a flattened bullet containing matted hair. He produced the bullet and made a diagram for the court. The court ordered that the bullet be weighed. It weighed 190 grains, about the weight of the .38-caliber slug.

Joe Allen, the operator of the beer garden near the Martha Rose Smelter at the edge of town, testified that the three men had stopped at his place for a beer. While Wilson and Mahar were drinking their beer, Cain went outside and discharged both of his guns. Wilson reached in his pocket and discovered that he had left his gun at home. He asked Allen if he could borrow a gun. Allen told him he didn't have a gun.

Drs. Lawrence, Brown, Presby, and Pascoe made the post-mortem examination. They testified that Wilson had been shot six times, with two balls entering the right side, one the left side, two entering the left side of the head (leaving severe powder burns), and one in the left forearm. Dr. Lawrence produced a bullet he had taken from Wilson's head. It weighed 195 grains.

Two witnesses who lived near Burro Bridge were called. D. J. Well said that he had heard four shots, the last two were fired together. L. S. Robertson, who also lives in a cabin near Burro Bridge, said that he had heard at least three shots, possibly more.

The next witness presented a damaging case against the defense. Mr. C. F. McCoin stated that he did not know Wilson but he did know Cain. He said that he had found three riderless horses heading for Silverton. He caught the horses and shortly after encountered Cain and Mahar on foot. He claimed that Cain remarked, "We got our man, all the same." Mahar countered with, "What's that?" Cain bragged, "Well at least I did."

The defense called Tom Cain to the stand. Tom's story was that he was in bed when his brother Pat and Phil Mahar came into his room. Pat told him that he had run into some trouble up the road and needed some .41 and .45-caliber cartridges. Tom said that he did not have any 41's but that he had a box of .45's he was welcome to use. He also told Pat to leave his .41-caliber gun and take Tom's .38-caliber pistol, which was loaded. After Pat and Phil told Tom what had happened, Tom suggested that they go to Billy Sullivan and give themselves up, which they did.

Several of Tom Cain's friends were trying to help with the cover-up, but many ended up contradicting each other. Tom testified that he had given Pat the .38-. H. A. Van Lugar, Tom's bartender, testified that he was the one who had given Pat the

.38. Butch Waggoner claimed he was present when Van Lugar exchanged Pat's .41 for the .38. Waggoner was a gambler working in Tom Cain's Blair Street dance hall. Several of Tom Cain's friends testified that they had heard Billy Wilson make brags that, "If he could get a show, he would kill both of those damn son-of-bitches." A gambler, James Collins, testified that when he was attending the February term of court at Gunnison, that Wilson told him, "Tom Cain had killed his best friend, Riley Lambert, and that he had taken a shot at Tom but had missed." A dance hall rustler, William Leonard, testified that Wilson had told him, "That he had just been waiting for the snow to go off so he could do up those Cains."

D. L. Mechling had weighed up for the court the two .41-caliber slugs taken from the body. He reported that one weighed 203 grains and the other 205 grains.

Finally, Sheriff Sullivan was called back to the stand. He told the court that Pat Cain had said nothing to him about exchanging guns. He said Cain gave Sullivan a .38 and a .45.

Most of the witnesses for the defense were part of Tom Cain's "gang." They were all bar owners, bartenders, gamblers or pimps. If what they said about Billy Wilson's threats to kill the Cains were true, it is highly unlikely that Wilson would be taking an early morning ride with the Cain clan without his gun.

Perhaps the most convincing testimony against Cain and Mahar, was the report by the two men who lived near the scene of the crime. One had heard three shots, "possibly more." The other had heard four, with the last two shots being fired together. Since there were six bullet holes in Wilson, this would indicate that Cain had fired both of his guns simultaneously twice, so as to sound like two shots instead of four. The last two shots were the final execution shots to Wilson's head.

The exchange of the guns story fabricated by Tom Cain, was to explain what happened to Pat Cain's .41-caliber pistol. Wilson was supposed to have borrowed Mahar's .41-pistol. Since they left a .41 next to the body, they were short a pistol. Actually, Mahar was carrying a .38-caliber gun. After Pat Cain murdered Billy Wilson, Phil Mahar finished him off with his .38. They left Pat's .41 behind to back up their very weak story. The two bullets that entered Wilson's head were .38's. They were not smart enough to leave the body were it fell. It is doubtful that a man with six bullet holes in him, including two through the head, is going to get up and move 30 paces carrying his gun with him. This was probably the most cold-blooded murder in the history of Silverton. The coroner's jury came to the same conclusion.

The people of Silverton were furious when Judge Bryant released Cain and Mahar on a light bail. Pat Cain's bond was set at $2,000 and Mahar's at $200. The bondsmen were Tom Cain, Joe Stender, a saloon owner, and John Murphy. The paper reported that "groups of men could be seen on every corner all day Monday discussing the matter. Sentiment of the community could not be misunderstood." One citizen reported that he knew for a fact that Judge Bryant had spent the night meeting secretly with Tom Cain. To further back the accusation that Bryant had been bribed, Pat Cain's friends from Rico went home that Saturday remarking to parties that they met on the road, "that everything was all right." Judge Bryant left town on Monday, "beastly drunk," for the Sheridan Mine in Marshall Basin where he was employed as an ore sorter. This tells something about the quality of early-day law in Silverton. The July 12, 1884, *Silverton Democrat*, printed the following article about Bryant:

> The best thing we have heard on Bryant was by Lawyer Gray. Monday evening Bryant rode up to his office on a mule and dismounted. While hitching the animal, it kept up a continuous braying, much to the annoyance of Bryant. Mr. Gray, who was standing nearby, noticed Bryant's discomfiture and called out to him, "That's the ghost of the murdered Wilson." Bryant made no reply, but sneaked into his office.

Shortly after Cain and Mahar were released on bail, the *Telluride Evening News*, printed the following story about their movements:

> Pat Cain and Phil Mahar were seen one day last week near the state line going in the direction of Utah. Both were mounted on fine horses and they were armed to the teeth. They also had a pack animal along which carried their blankets, etc. It is supposed they were taking a French leave.

The editor of the *Silverton Democrat*, Mr. H. M. Condict, wrote the story of the Wilson murder as he, and most everyone in town, saw it, based on the testimony of the above witnesses. Tom Cain, in a fit of temper, vowed "to 'fix' Condict if he ever mentioned Tom's or Pat Cain's name in his damned paper again." Condict continued to print the story at the risk of his life.

On the night of August 8, 1884, Editor Condict was having a drink with Dick Journey, the mine superintendent of the National Belle Mine, at M. K. Cohen's Arion Hall (Fig. 53) Tom Cain entered with a gang of his henchmen. One of the gang, a man by the name of "Dutchy," picked a fight with Jacob Schaefor and was "abusing him shamefully." Condict remarked to Journey that he would like to see "Dutchy" get licked. Tom Cain overheard the remark, and immediately his gang surrounded Condict and Journey at their table. Cain collared Condict with the remark, "By God, maybe you would like to do it." Cain held Condict by the collar, and began abusing him for the stories he had printed about the Cain-Mahar murder trial. In the course of the threats, Cain told Condict, "If you ever mention Tom Cain's name or my brothers in your God damn paper again, there will be one Jim Crow editor that'll not write anything more." Condict and Journey were at a great disadvantage, being pinned in their chairs, they could do nothing. Shortly after Cain and his gang left, Condict and Journey started home. They were crossing the street between the bank and Stender & Ryan's place when Cain called to them to stop. They stopped. Cain and his gang started to rough them up again when the town policeman arrived on the scene. Cain told Policeman Kilbourne that if he had not been present it would have been much worse for Condict.

Condict immediately printed the story of Cain's threats in his paper. He stated that, "Tom Cain has promised to 'fix' us if his or his brother's name is ever again mentioned in the *Democrat*. It is consoling to know that we will not be the first he has ever 'fixed.' He also called on the good people of Silverton to drive men like Cain out of town. He reminded his readers that:

> This same Tom Cain has passed as a 'badman' ever since he has been in the country; he is the man who fired into a crowd at Silver Cliff in 1878 and killed an innocent man for which he has never been tried; he is the man who killed Riley Lambert; he is the man who has made several uncalled for gun plays in Silverton; he is the man upon whom suspicion rests heavily on account of the murder of Wilson; he is the man who runs a dance hall and keeps a woman, and he is the infamous cur that seeks to stifle public opinion by threats of violence and intimidations.

Editor Condict was an extremely courageous man. Even the Denver press printed articles commending his brave actions.

Shortly after the above threats by Cain, Condict filed a formal complaint against Cain for threatening his life. The case went to trial and Cain was found guilty. Justice Earl heard the case and released Tom Cain on a $300 bond. The other witnesses were to put up a $150 bond to assure that they would show up for the district court trial. Condict was elated that the courts finally found Cain guilty of something. He didn't think that the $300 bail would deter Cain from leaving the country if he wanted, but at least he hoped that it would teach Cain that he could not muzzle the press. He wrote in his August 16 issue, "We shall write up Mr. Cain, or Mr. Smith, or Mr. Brown, or Mr. Jones whenever we feel so disposed and shall say exactly what our judgment dictates is right, without fear of favor."

H. M. Condict won a moral victory over Tom Cain; however, the bond set by Judge Earl was never put up. In a comedy scene of early Silverton law, Judge Earl was called up by the district court to explain why the bond was not paid. The following direct testimony of the court reveals the lax nature of 1884 law.

The summary of the court's censure of Justice W. E. Earl was printed in the September 6, 1884, *Silverton Democrat*:

Justice W. E. Earl

'Mr. Earl, please take the stand."

'Mr. Earl, do you remember of having heard a case on or about August 11, 1884, wherein the people of the State of Colorado were plaintiffs and Thomas Cain defendant?'

'Yes sir.'

'Can you now call to mind the result of that trial?'

'Yes, I held the defendant under $300 bond and the state witnesses under $150 each.'

'Now, Mr. Earl, will you please state to the court (the people) whether the bonds of the state witnesses were ever required or not?'

'They were not.'

'Yes, Well, now did or did not Mr. Condict, the prosecuting witness, call upon you on more than one occasion for the purpose of furnishing his required bond?'

'He did.'

'Was the bond of defendant Cain, ever required?'

'It was not.'

'Did you deliver to the District Court the proceedings of this case as your are required by law to do?'

'I did not.'

'And can you give any satisfactory explanation of your actions in this matter—the palpable neglect of many of your duties as a Justice of the Peace?'

Just here a dogfight occurred in front of the *Democrat* office and the witness was so much interested that he adjourned himself and we have been unable to get him on the stand since.

However, the use of our columns are hereby tendered the gentleman for the purpose of giving his answer to an anxious constituency.

Condict collected items from the Denver press about his heroic stand against the Cain gang. He was quick to print the comments of the "State" press. "The State press is unanimous in its praise of the *Democrat's* fearless denunciation of Tom Cain and his layout."

Editor Condict was furious over Judge Bryant's release of Pat Cain and Phil Mahar on such a light bond. As was expected, both Cain and Mahar skipped town and were never captured. Condict wrote the following plea to the governor in the September 6, 1884, *Silverton Democrat*: "The governor should at once offer a large reward for the apprehension of Pat Cain and Phil Mahar, the murderers of Billy Wilson."

Condict continued his assault on Justice Bryant. It is obvious that libel suits were not the "in thing" during the 1880's. He wrote, on September 6, 1884, the following:

It is believed that an earnest effort was made by the grand jury to find sufficient evidence to indict the late Justice Cushing M. Bryant of bribery. No doubt of his guilt rests in the mind of any man acquainted with the circumstances, but it is an impossible matter to get positive evidence.

Editor Condict's efforts to obtain justice against Tom Cain were finally rewarded. Cain was not only indicted for threatening Condict's life, but also for a shooting spree which occurred during the summer in the Fashion Saloon.

Tom Cain Indicted

We take great pleasure in informing the few remaining friends of Tom Cain, that we have pretty straight information of the gentleman's indictment by the grand jury this week. A true bill was found against Thomas for his little gunplay on Fatty Collins at the Fashion Saloon in the early part of the summer. Thus, 'one by one the roses fall'—when they monkey with the editor.

When Pat Cain and Phillip Mahar jumped bail and left the country, the bondsmen were left owing the county $2,200. Tom Cain, along with the other bondsmen, suggested that the county take Cain's dance hall in lieu of the $2,200 bond. The attorneys for the people consulted several real estate people and the consensus was that Tom Cain's Blair Street dance hall was worth $3,000. Mr. Stender, one of the bondholders, suggested that the county issue $400 in county script to the three bondholders to offset the difference between the required bond and the higher value of the dance hall. This deal was accepted against complaints of the *Democrat*, that the property was only worth $1,500 at best. It would be better to get the $1,500 than nothing, which is what they would have received from Cain and the other bondholders in a year's time.

To make a long story short, the town of Silverton ended up owning Tom Cain's Saloon and Dance Hall on the southeast corner of 13th and Blair Streets. At one time, they moved the town offices into his building. Thus, one of Blair Street's early bordellos became the local offices for the Town of Silverton.

Tom Cain lost his saloon and dance hall and immediately left Silverton for the Arizona Territory. He moved to Ashfork and opened another dance hall. It was rumored that his brother Pat was living with him. News of the following nature reached Silverton:

October 4, 1884, *Silverton Democrat*:

Information was received in Silverton this week that one more unfortunate has met, at the hands of the Cain outfit, that peculiar treatment known as 'fixing.' In other words, about the 20th of last month, at Ashfork, A. T. (Arizona Territory) it is currently rumored that (Tom and Pat Cain) got into a slight altercation with a miner at that place and deliberately shot him dead. Further particulars we have been unable to learn.

Shortly after the above article was received, Tom Cain met his equal and the old adage that "he who lives by the gun, dies, by the gun" came true.

Tom Cain Reported Killed

Mr. Robert Roberts, of this city, received yesterday a telegram from

Ashfork, A. T., and signed by Wm. Leonard, which stated that Tom Cain was killed in that place the night before. We have been unable to obtain further particulars up to the hour of going to press. Tom Cain, it will be remembered, formerly ran a dance hall in this place; shot Riley Lambert November 25th last year and his skirts were not entirely clear of the Wilson murder. His reputation was very bad throughout southern Colorado, where he was well known.

December 6, 1884, *Silverton Democrat:*

The Cain Homicide

There now seems little doubt that Tom Cain has 'passed in his checks.' There was much doubt in the minds of many as to whether the Leonard telegram was genuine and correct. That telegram arrived about noon Thursday, the 27th, and stated 'Tom Cain was killed at 1 o'clock this morning.' The suspicion that this telegram was bogus was greatly strengthened on Thursday of this week, when Mattie Cook received a letter from her sister who lives in Albuquerque, stating that it is 'Jim' Marshall who was killed in Ashfork, A. T., on Thanksgiving morning. Later in the same day that Mattie Cook received her letter, William Snyder received a telegram from M. B. ('Jim') Marshall. The telegram was as follows, and was sent in answer to a letter of inquiry addressed to Marshall, immediately after the first news of Cain's murder was received:

'Ashfork, A. T., December 4, 1884, ---Just received your letter, Leonard's dispatch is correct. I was in Prescott at the time. He was shot on the 27th of November. Got 18 buckshot in his breast. Was shot by a teamster by the name of Evans, who got clear.'

Signed: M. B. Marshall

The article continued:

From the above it would appear that the man Evans was justified in what he did. From all we can gather the circumstances are as follows: Cain and Marshall were running a sort of variety show and dance hall at Ashfork. It was after the show and during the dance that Cain got into trouble with Evans over eighty cents. Cain began his characteristic bluster, accompanied by his promise to 'do him (Evans) up.' Evans told him he was unarmed and Cain then said: 'Well, go and fix yourself, and that God damn quick, too, and I'll settle this matter with you.' It appears that the man went out and procured a heavily loaded double-barreled shotgun and returned to the dance hall. Just as he stepped in the door he called to Cain. 'Are you ready?' Cain replied 'yes' and reached for his gun. As Cain turned fairly facing Evans, the latter discharged both barrels of his gun at once. Eighteen buckshot taking effect in his breast as stated in the telegram quoted above. Cain fired one shot as he fell, it going through the ceiling. Evans gave himself up and was cleared at the preliminary examination.

So ends the story of Tom Cain, one of Silverton's earliest saloon and dance hall operators.

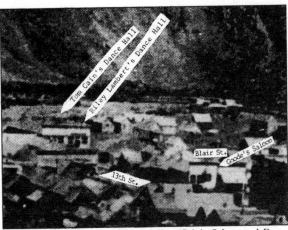

Fig. 51. **Then**-1884 photo showing Tom Cain's Saloon and Dance Hall. Riley Lambert's Saloon is next door. Cain's Saloon was on the southeast corner of 13th and Blair Streets (Colo. Hist. Society photo)

Fig. 52. **Now**-1883 jail now stands on the site of Tom Cain's Saloon. (Allan G. Bird-May, 1999 photo)

Fig. 53. **Then**-July 4, 1885 photo showing M. K. Cohen's Arion Saloon (3rd from right) where Tom Cain roughed up Editor Condict in 1884. East side of Greene Street, between 12th and 13th Streets. Silverton's early Cornet Band. (San Juan Co. Hist. Society photo)

Fig. 54. **Now**-Arion Saloon stood in the space now occupied by the right side of the Teller House. The Teller House was built in 1896. East side of Greene Street, between 12th and 13th Streets. (Allan G. Bird photo-May, 1999)

In 1884, Ed Gorman sold out his interest in the Tivoli Saloon and moved across the street to a frame false-front (lot now occupied by leather shop north of Teller House), where he opened the Turf Exchange Saloon (Fig. 53). Gorman was well liked in Silverton but his wife was another story. She served as a singer in his saloon and probably came from one of the bordellos of Silverton. The "proper" ladies of Silverton would have nothing to do with her. Gorman, prospering somewhat in his business, decided to move to Quality Hill, on the west edge of town. This was the center of Silverton's society circles. Mrs. Gorman frequently imbibed in the juice, which caused her to become rather loud and boisterous. From time to time, she would go out and soil the pristine ears of her royal neighbors with some choice words. The *Silverton Democrat* took issue with her behavior writing the following article:

> Something must be done. Mrs. Gorman was making a general nuisance again yesterday afternoon, indulging in her usual boisterous and indecent language, greatly to the annoyance and disgust of the ladies living in the immediate vicinity. Such occurrences will soon drive away every family from that locality. In fact, today, Mr. Fleming is moving his family. This is a grave state of affairs and it lies with the city council to remedy it speedily.

The cross was raised over the new Catholic church on Reese Street, north of 10th, on September 6, 1883 (Fig. 55). This church served the Catholic members of Silverton until 1905. It was sold to the African Methodist-Episcopal Congregation and moved to Mineral Street. A new Catholic church was built on the northwest corner of Reese and 10th Streets and serves the community to this day.

Fig. 55. **Then**-1883 Catholic church. Used until 1905. Sold to the African Methodist-Episcopal Church and moved to Mineral Street. 1884 photo. (San Juan Co. Hist. Society photo)

On September 6, 1883, the controversial Col. J. M. Chivington visited the Congregational church. He was the perpetrator of the infamous San Creek Massacre against the Cheyenne Indians on November 24, 1864. Chivington and his First Colorado Regiment slaughtered helpless women, children, and old men in their camp along Sand Creek. Most of the young men were out on a hunting party when the raid took place. As late as 1883, Chivington was considered a hero in the eyes of Colorado citizens. The *La Plata Miner* reviewed the talk and wrote the following comments:

> The atrocities that preceded the battle and which had been committed by the Indians were not half told, they could not be within the hearing of delicate ears, still enough was recited to convince all of those present of the righteousness of the terrible vengeance that was visited upon the hostiles at Sand Creek. The lecture was well attended and, the only good trait most noticeable about the Col. is that he killed 700 papooses. 'knits breed lice.'

On October 23, 1883, the new town water reservoir was filled and the water turned on. The system was privately owned. Construction had been postponed by city hall red tape concerning the method of financing. About a year earlier in January, the paper bragged, "We ain't troubled with having water pipes frozen up over here in Silverton." An obvious dig against the city fathers for their lack of action on a water system.

1884 arrived with the usual turnover of business establishments. Kinnan Farnsworth Hardware Company (in the Grand Hotel building) became Kinnan Harris & Company. The town boasted of a host of businesses, plus 29 saloons and 5000 dogs. The dog problem was a constant topic of discussion in the local papers. "The dogs continue in the majority. A vigilance committee is necessary to insure their perfect happiness."

On February 2, 1884, a severe snowstorm blocked the railroad and cut off all supplies to Silverton (Figs. 56 & 57). The heavy snows also destroyed one of the original Greene Street buildings. Snow slid from the roof of Tom Blair's two-story business building, two doors north of the Grand Hotel, (Figs. 58 & 59) and crushed the roof of the adjoining Lafayette Restaurant building. Blair had completed this building about mid-June, 1883. The old restaurant building had recently been undergoing repairs preparatory to its occupation by the St. Julien Restaurant. On March 15, the area suffered another storm, thus extending the railroad blockade.

The new St. Julien building, replacing the Lafayette Restaurant, was a two-story frame completed in late March, 1884. This building remains today (Fig. 60.)

By March 22, the blockade had lasted 49 days. H. P. Walton was forced out of business by the long snow siege. He had liabilities of $30,000 and assets of $15,000. The failure was caused by a combination of too much credit and no money to pay the creditors. Ore could not be transported to the smelters and money was scarce. The train finally arrived on April 9, after 73 days.

Greene Street looking north from 12th Street is well illustrated in the photo (Fig. 61) taken about April, 1885. Tom Blair's new business building (not the

Fig. 56. **Then**-Snow blockade of the railroad similar to the 1884 blockade which lasted 73 days. Photo taken in 1932. (Jim Bell photo)

Fig. 57. **Then**-1929 snow blockade. Two engines used to buck the deep snow. (Jim Bell Photo)

Fig. 58. **Then**-1901 photo showing Tom Blair's 1883 building, left of center, and the new 1884 St. Julien building that replace the St. Julien Restaurant that was destroyed by snow falling off of Blair's roof. Both buildings later became known as the Lacy buildings. Building on the right was built in 1888, known as the Perrung building, later occupied by the Silverton Supply Company. The building was destroyed by snow in the mid-1970's. (Colo. Hist. Soc. Photo)

Fig. 59. **Now**-Tom Blair's 1883 building in August, 1998. (Allan G. Bird photo)

Fig. 60. **Now**-1989 photo of the 1884 "new" St. Julien Restaurant building, later one of the Lacy buildings. (Allan G. Bird photo)

Fig. 61. **Then**-1885 view of Greene Street looking north from 12th Street. All but one of the buildings on the right side (the liquor side) of Greene Street has been replaced. Only the 1880 stone Sherwin building remains (Pickle Barrel Restaurant). (Ruth Gregory photo)

Fig. 62. **Now**-August, 1998 photo of Greene Street looking north from 12th Street. Same scene as Fig. 61. (Allan G. Bird photo)

Assembly Rooms) is the tall white building on the left just beyond the awning. The new St. Julien Restaurant building, adjacent to Blair's on the north, was completed in May, 1884. Dave Lowenstein opened a wholesale liquor store in the front of the St. Julien Restaurant; the restaurant was in the rear of the building. J. L. Stanley occupied the small building with the awning as a fruit-news stand and circulating library, until December, 1884. At that time, Ottis Ballou moved in with his restaurant. Stanley moved into the St. Julien Restaurant and the St. Julien moved into the Grand Hotel. The barber pole in front of the Grand Hotel building helps date the photo. Casper Malchus, the barber, moved into Brett's vacated store in the hotel on September 11, 1884 and moved out on July 11, 1885.

On the east side of Greene Street, known as the liquor side, there were thirteen businesses, ten were saloons, gambling halls or houses of prostitution. On the far right was Jane and William Bowen's Westminster Hall, probably Silverton's first saloon-brothel. The rear of the building had two stories, the upper story for the girls. In 1880, the Bowen's built a large two-story frame building directly behind Westminster Hall. This was originally their residence. When prostitution was outlawed on Greene Street in late 1884, they expanded the building and moved their operation to Blair Street.

William Bowen came to Silverton in 1875 and was probably one of the wealthiest men in town. He was taxed at the same level as the Greene & Company store and smelter. At one time he invested $10,000 in a mine on Sultan Mountain, a fortune at that time. His wife Jane, known as "Aunt Jane" or the "Sage Hen" ran the saloon and girls.

Next door to Bowen's, to the north was a small 25 foot-wide slot in which a tent roof was put up and a small fruit stand established. In June, 1885, the town fire department built a small, enclosed building to house the fire hose cart.

The next building north was a saloon, whose ownership is unknown.

The building with the sign "Silverton Bargain House" was moved onto the lot from a location on 13th Street on July 3, 1884. T. P. Head opened the Bargain House a month later.

Col. Francis M. Snowden built the taller building, just to the upper right of the covered wagon, as an investment in early August, 1882. Snowden rented the building to J. H. Brink, owner of the Metropolitan Saloon. Brink was the late Marshal Ogsbury's mining partner in 1879, and later replaced Ogsbury as town marshal. He moved the Metropolitan to this location from the upstairs of the Posey & Wingate brick building across the street to the north. In August, 1884, Brink sold half interest in his saloon to Harry LeRoy, also a law officer.

The next building down the row was rented by Tom Cain, Silverton's Town Marshal at the time. In April, 1884, Cain leased the building to Adolphus Schnebelen, who operated the Adolphus Beer Hall. In late October, 1885, Adolphus Schnebelen sold his Beer Hall and moved into Mrs. Cotton's 13th Street rental (Fig. 66), where he opened the Adolphus Restaurant.

The tallest building on the block is the Fashion Saloon and Theater, also called the Fashion Concert Hall. By August, 1884, the Fashion changed hands.

Beyond the Fashion was a small saloon operated by Plunket and Cleary (Fig. 50) in 1884 and probably 1885.

The next tall building is the Exchange Livery, (Fig. 50), built by Herr, Hodges, and Herr, July 7, 1881. Hodges sold out to a gentleman by the name of Bradford on November 11, 1884, changing the name to Herr, Bradford, & Herr. The livery was a two story wooden frame covering one 25 foot-wide lot.

The building next door to the livery was leased to M. K. Cohen shortly after he had been released from prison. Cohen named his saloon the "Arion," (Fig. 50) which was discussed in the Tom Cain story. He opened the saloon on August 1, 1884. By December, 1884, his usual luck was holding true and he went broke. In early May, 1885, Koehler & Higgs reopened the Arion.

Beyond the Arion was Robert Robert's Saloon and Bowling Alley (Fig. 50).

Next door to the north, was Ed Gorman's Turf Exchange Saloon (Fig. 50).

On the corner, was the old Goode & Rousche's Senate Saloon. The late Marshal Ogsbury lived in the rear of this building. Stender and Ryan now ran the saloon. Stender was one of the bondsmen for Pat Cain and Phil Mahar.

On the night of June 27, 1885, Jim Stacy, a miner, was held up at gunpoint on Greene Street, between the "Sage Hen's" Westminster Hall and Harry LeRoy's Metropolitan Saloon. Two men held a gun on him and robbed him of 25 cents, all the money he had at the time. The following day, Marshal Tom Sewall, who was filling in for Marshal George Seaman while Seaman was visiting his sick father, noticed two suspicious-looking characters casing Kinnan's Hardware Store in the Grand Hotel. (Kinnan's was located in the present bar and dining room of the Grand Imperial Hotel). On a hunch, Sewall notified the store manager, Pete Breicheisen, and told him that he suspected that the store would be robbed that evening. The marshal and Brecheisen laid out a plan whereby they would hide in a small bedroom located below the stairs leading to the upper floors of the hotel. (Now hidden behind the south wall of the hotel barroom). They lit an oil lamp. Brecheisen was to keep the light covered with his hat until Sewall nudged him with his foot. On the signal, he was to lift the hat so Sewall could get the drop on the burglar with his double-barreled shotgun. They arrived at the store about 9:30 p. m. and waited patiently in the dark. Shortly after 10 p. m., they heard an oil can fall in the rear of the store. They spotted the shadow of the burglar but it was too dark to see exactly where he was. After a few minutes, Sewall kicked Breicheisen, who quickly lifted his hat from the lantern, forcing the lantern to go out. Since they were both in a precarious position, Sewall let go with one barrel of the shotgun in the direction of the sound. They heard a voice cry out, "I'm shot."

After re-lighting the lantern, they found the buckshot-riddled body of C. L. Godfrey lying on the floor. Five Colt revolvers were strung on a piece of rope beneath his body. Godfrey was the same man that Sewall had observed during the day. Later, Jim Stacy identified him as the man who had robbed him of 25 cents the night before. The papers later criticized Sewall, saying that he wanted to make a name for himself by killing someone. He violated the code-of-the-west by shooting first and asking questions later.

In late September, 1885, M. K. Cohen, along with John Walter, purchased the Grand Hotel Saloon, which was located in the basement of the hotel. How Cohen kept coming up with capital is a mystery. In late November, the partnership dissolved and Walters took over the saloon. Cohen was again out of work.

In November, Billy Cole moved his boarding house from the old Montgomery Brother's Store to the old Centennial Hotel (Grand Central Hotel). Over the coming years, Cole was to establish the longevity record for any Silverton businessman.

Governor Eaton granted Frank McMillian, the villain who bilked the widow and five children out of their life savings, a full pardon from the penitentiary. He was pardoned on the recommendation of the judge who sentenced him and other citizens of Silverton. Silverton seemed to be very forgiving of their felons.

In late October, 1884, the would-be musicians of Silverton decided that the town needed a brass band. The *Silverton Democrat* unleashed its feelings in the October 25 issue with the following comments:

> About a dozen of our town boys meet nightly in the brick adjoining the *Democrat* office. They have a number of instruments and are trying to make a brass band out of themselves, but they have been more successful thus far in making heathens out of the residents in the vicinity.

About a month later, the *La Plata Miner* wrote:

> 'The music rendered by the Silverton Cornet Band on the streets Thursday was very creditable for such a new organization.' The *Miner* was not so kind the following April when it wrote: 'The new band has as yet learned to play but one tune, and that is all in one note. Boycott it! Put it in a snowslide! Across the way from the *Miner* office it is located.

'Music hath charms to soothe, but this don't soothe.'

Fig. 53 shows the band in the July 4, 1885, parade.

Excitement came in early 1886. In late January, one of Silverton's rare murders took place in Gorman & Roe's Turf Exchange Saloon (Fig. 53). About half-past seven in the evening. John Barnet, known as Arkansaw (Sic) John, had placed a bet of two silver dollars on the faro table. After losing, he reached in his pocket and placed a five-dollar bill on the number. L. F. Toles had lent John some money, which John had never repaid. When Toles saw the five dollars, he reached over and grabbed the money. John told him to put it back. When Toles refused, a scuffle took place. They clinched and Toles bit Arkansaw, over the right eye. Arkansaw reached in his pocket and took out his penknife, stabbing Toles in the heart. Toles let loose, staggered, and fell into a chair. Someone yelled to go for a doctor. Arkansaw volunteered, leaving by the front door in search of the doctor. The sheriff and marshal were notified, and arrived on the scene shortly after Arkansaw had left. They immediately sent out a search party for him. He was found by Mr. Malchus, the barber, walking in front of Tom Blair's old Assembly Rooms (then occupied by Malchus). Mr. Malchus was also a deputy sheriff. He exercised his powers and put Arkansaw under arrest. He took him across the street and held him in Fred Sherwin's stone store. Toles was laid out on a stud poker table, where he died a short time after the stabbing. Arkansaw had been in Silverton since 1876. He and Toles had been the best of friends. A trial was held and Arkansaw was sentenced to two years and nine months at Canon City. A few years after his release, he himself was killed in Pitkin, Colorado during a saloon fight over gambling. Toles was 35 years old.

As one might guess, the saloons of Silverton were rough places. A week after Toles was murdered, a man by the name of "Red" raised a ruckus in the Metropolitan Saloon and had his arm broken by a poker wielded by the bartender.

In March, 1886, Frank Cooper moved the Hub Saloon (Fig. 63) into the Grand Hotel (present hotel lobby). The Hub began business on August 2, 1883, in

Fig. 63. **Then**-1901 photo showing the Hub Saloon sign, in front of the hotel awning. (Colorado Historical Society photo)

the room behind the First National Bank (located in the rear of the Posey & Wingate two-story brick building). The bank, originally formed as the San Juan National Bank, changed its name to the First National Bank on May 21, 1883.

On December 5, 1885, about a year before the Hub moved to its new location, the *La Plata Miner* reported the story of the knifing of the proprietor of the Hub Saloon on 13th Street:

> The tracks of blood leading from the Hub Saloon along Thirteenth Street were the subject of much comment on Monday morning, and from the quantity of blood spilled, it really seemed as though some one had bled to death. Subsequent inquiry elicited the facts that Frank Cooper, the proprietor of the Hub, had been cut in the hand while in the act of defending himself from an enraged woman, who sprang at him with a clasp knife. Frank caught the knife, and as the blade was drawn through, it left an ugly gash in the palm of his hand. The difficulty had begun in the Fashion when it is said that Frank refused to dance with the woman, Nell Castell, and she then followed him to the saloon with the results stated.

Nell Castell was the owner of one of Blair Street's larger bordellos. We will hear more about her in Chapter 4.

The Hub became a Silverton landmark until it was closed by Prohibition in January, 1916. National Prohibition did not occur until January 16, 1920, but Colorado jumped the gun by four years. After Prohibition, the Hub operated as a soft drink center and pool hall until its demise in January, 1920.

In late March, 1886, The Fashion Saloon was leased to Koehler & Higgs for three years. They bought the saloon fixtures from the Arlington Saloon, which was now defunct. M. K. Cohen, now in the sign painting and decorating business, painted a drop curtain for the Fashion, which was "the finest piece of artistic lettering done in Silverton."

On the first of May, the post office was moved one door north (to the southwest corner of 14th and Greene Streets). The old Luesley store, later Matthews and Walton's, was remodeled and leased for four years. The new paper, *The San Juan*, moved into the old post office building. As late as November 11, the paper reported that: "An average of three persons a day come in wanting to know where the post office has moved to." Not too smart.

Otto Mears, the builder of the original toll roads into Silverton, was constructing the new road to Red Mountain Town, toward Ouray. The *Denver Journal of Commerce* reported that he had the heaviest wagon in the U. S., weighing 20,000 tons. Mears replied:

> Vot dot tam fool toldt such a story vor? I shust have Fred Valsen
> go und hexplain dot we can't run a steamboat to dot Red Mountain.
> Dwenty tousnad tons! Oh, Sheminie!

Joseph Bordeleau, a Canadian, rented the Silverton Skating Rink (two doors to the north of the Brown Bear Restaurant-Fig 64). He moved in on the first of May, 1886. In August, his store was broken into and the safe blown. The thieves got away with $75 plus a gold nugget worth $22. The thieves, Paul Kelly and "High Ball Pete," were quickly apprehended, tried and sentenced to five and eight years respectively in Canon City. They were turned in to the "foreman of the rock breakers."

Fig. 64. **Then**-1908 photo showing Joseph Bordeleau's Hardware Store, right of center. (Eddie Lorenzon photo)

Fig. 65. **Now**-New 1998 building on site of Bordeleau's Hardware Store. The *Silverton Standard* newspaper occupies the second store from the left. (Allan G. Bird-August, 1998 photo)

The local pressure on Ed Gorman and his vociferous wife finally came to a head in late October. Gorman sold his interest in the Turf Exchange Saloon to Fuqua & McCurdy. He moved to Durango and opened the Gold Room Saloon.

On November 24, 1886, Buffalo Bill's Wild West Show was on exhibition for three hours. No mention was made of whether they put on a show.

As a sideline, M. K. Cohen went into the raffle business. He offered 300 chances at a dollar a chance. The drawing was to take place at George Seaman's Arion Saloon on New Year's Eve. Five prizes, consisting of a diamond ring, a gold watch, a gold chain, a gold set ring, and a set of gold cuff buttons were offered. Three hundred dollars could buy a lot of gold in the "good-old days." The year, 1887, started off quietly with M. K. Cohen leaving for Kansas City to travel for a wholesale liquor house.

In early March, George Fleming, and his partner, Mechling, sold their drug store stock to George Bayly's Post Office Drug Store. This cut the drug store population down to two, B. A. Taft's on Reese Street and Bayly's on Greene. On April 1, Taft moved to the empty store, next door to the south, of the Hub Saloon in the Grand Hotel building. This was the old Kinnan Hardware Store. Mrs. Reed and Miss Dell Jackson moved their R-J Restaurant into Fleming's building on the first of April.

The Kansas City wholesale liquor business did not suit M. K. Cohen; he returned March 10 to reopen his painting business. His advertisements read: "sign and ornamental painting."

The anti-Indian sentiment was well illustrated by the *Silverton Democrat's* editorial reported on March 26, 1887. It read:

> Mr. R. H. Rohrig (the butcher) returned from the southern country on Wednesday. The Indians had killed 45 of his sheep and run off with 155 more. This outrage was perpetrated by the Navajos during the transfer of the heard of 4000 from Utah to the summer range near Pagosa. The same Indians had killed a sheepherder about two weeks ago. Uncle Sam's wards are delightful people. They ought to be transferred to New England, where they are loved so much.

In late April, "Billy" Cole, proprietor of the Centennial Rooming House, returned from Durango with a team of horses. He combined the boarding house with the express wagon business.

The spring of 1887 brought harder times to Silverton than previous years. The town fathers raised the saloon license fee for all-night saloons to $300. The paper complained, "$300 today is harder to come by than $600 a few years ago." At the same time, they ordained: "Women of easy virtue will hereafter not be allowed to parade the streets, visit the saloons, or ride on horseback on any of the streets west of Blair."

Early May revealed a classic case of law enforcement in Silverton. It seems that Mr. John Smith was arrested for burglarizing Mrs. Bat's Hotel. He was released on a technicality because the complaint was not drawn up properly. Smith was again arrested for robbing Al Wiley, clerk of the Grand Hotel. Wiley lost $53 from his coat pocket, which was taken from his locked room in the hotel. Suspicion pointed toward Smith. Upon searching Smith, they found a five-cent piece on his person, which Wiley immediately identified as his. He was brought to trial and sentenced to a term in the State Penitentiary at Canon City. It must have been one uncommon nickel.

On June 1, Jerry Ryan, the owner of the old Goode & Rousche's Senate Saloon, died suddenly. His wife was out of town and could not return for several days. They packed him in ice until her arrival.

The St. Charles Restaurant had recently moved into Mrs. Cotton's frame building on the north side of 13th Street (between Reese and Greene). The photo (Fig. 66), looking toward the west, shows a row of small buildings adjacent to the St. Charles, which were occupied by offices and millinery stores. The old B. A. Taft 1875 drug store is seen on the corner facing the camera. Note Taft's signs have all been painted over, awaiting a new tenant. Taft had painted the front of his vacant store during the last week of August. The photo is dated early September, 1887. It is an excellent scene showing the burro trains hauling rail to the mines along with an ore car. The old San Juan Herald building is visible on the far left. The St. Charles Restaurant and the adjoining building burned to the ground in June, 1888. The building was at one time occupied by the Adolphus Restaurant and later by the Delmonico Restaurant. Figure 64 shows this same scene today (1998).

In September, 1887, Joseph Dixon, a mulatto who had run the Delmonico Restaurant, was in Ouray. Dixon had worked with 24 year-old Nellie Day at the Beaumont Hotel in that city. He had a fight with the girl that ended in Dixon shooting her at close range, killing her instantly. He was immediately arrested and taken to the town jail. That night a mob advanced against the jail and tried to break in but failed. They then wrapped the jail in blankets, soaked with kerosene. After the fire was put out, Dixon was found "roasted to death" in his cell.

July 4, 1887 was celebrated by the arrival of John Robinson's Great World Exposition Circus. It took 60 railroad cars to carry the circus to Silverton. The Silverton Cornet Band provided the music for the celebration.

R. H. Rohrig, in addition to owning flocks of sheep and herds of cattle, decided to raise fish in Silverton. He owned a ranch on the land now covered by the reclaimed tailing ponds north of town. He built a series of ponds beside the river. An agreement was made with the State Fish Hatchery for Rohrig to buy 20,000 small trout for his project. The paper noted:

> There is an iron spring just at the edge of the creek in which the fish are located, and in a deep hole into which the water from the iron spring runs, the fish will congregate in great numbers. So that Mr. Rohrig has come to the conclusion that fish are not adversed to mineral water.

His fish thrived for four years and were ready for market when a cloudburst washed out one of his dams and the entire population of 20,000 trout ended up in the Animas River.

Speaking of pollution, Quong Wah, owner of a Chinese laundry, was fined $10 plus $7 costs for dumping soapsuds into the town ditches.

Fig. 66. **Then**-1887 photo looking west along the north side of 13th Street, between Greene and Reese Streets. The Cotton building,, housing the St. Charles Restaurant, burned in June, 1888. (Eddie Lorenzon photo)

Fig. 67. **Now**-The north side of 13th Street today. All the buildings shown in Fig. 66 are now gone. (Allan G. Bird photo-August, 1998)

Professional prizefights provided a common form of entertainment in old Silverton. In early November, 1887, two undefeated fighters were booked into the Alhambra Theater (on Blair Street, located on the lot where the Shady Lady Restaurant now stands). Johnson and Slatterly were the contestants. A few days before the scheduled fight, Slatterly became obnoxious while drinking in the Metropolitan Saloon. Ex-mayor Snowden told him to quiet down. Slatterly swung at Snowden. Snowden ducked and promptly decked him "in two rounds." Slatterly required several stitches over his eye. The scheduled bare-knuckle fight was fought to a draw after over twenty rounds.

January, 1888, started with a fire in the Congregational church. A faulty furnace burned the floor and rug. The insurance company adjusted for the damage and $218 was paid for repairs. It was decided to do away with the central furnace and install a series of small stoves.

On March 1, 1888, "Billy" Cole, who had moved to Ouray the previous September, returned and opened a small restaurant in the building formerly occupied by Akkola & Perrung as a bakery and restaurant. This was the old 1875 Brown & Cort Saloon building. Akkola and Perrung moved down the street into the old B. W. Thayer Mercantile Company's building, (on the lot now occupied by the Silverton Mineral's and Gift Shop). They moved into the building on March 3rd. About a week later, the building burned to the ground. Miraculously, the adjoining buildings were saved. It was 24 degrees below zero during the fire. Akkola and Perrung immediately began construction on a new building. This structure lasted until the 1970's, when snow caved in the roof. (The present Silverton Minerals and Gift Shop was built in 1983 and is the only new building on the block.)

Fig. 68. **Then**-Billy Cole's new men's furnishing store. (Old Arlington Saloon building) Cole moved into this building on April 1, 1890. (Patty Dailey photo)

On April 1, 1890, Billy Cole sold his restaurant to the Livingston Brothers and moved next door to the south into the old Arlington Saloon building (Fig 68). He remained in this building until 1901 when he tore down the old building and built, along with his friend, Fritz Hoffman, the large two-story brick and stone building (Fig. 69) which now dominates the west side of Greene Street between 13th and 14th Streets.

Cole remained in that location until his death on March 7, 1932. He was 80 years old at the time of his death and had been in the store hours before he died.

Fig. 69. **Now**-Billy Cole's stone building completed in 1902 on site of his old frame store. (Allan G. Bird-August, 1998 photo)

Construction began on the Red Mountain Railroad in June, 1888. The *San Juan Democrat* stated:

> Yesterday's train brought in another load of Dago laborers for the Red Mountain Railroad. The platform looked for a while, on a small scale, like Castle Garden on the arrival of a large ocean steamer from some foreign country.

The Italian members of the community, rightly so, took offense at this reference. The paper replied that they could see nothing wrong in referring to Italians affectionately as "Dagos." Times do change.

Fig. 70. **Then**-H. G. Prosser's new 1888 Crane & Breed Hearse. Cost-$1,000. (San Juan Co. Historical Society photo)

H. G. Prosser, the town undertaker, purchased a new hearse directly from the manufacturer, Crane & Breed of Cincinnati, Ohio (Fig. 70). The paper reported: "Our dead can now be buried decently instead of being hauled in a rude express wagon." (Prosser's establishment was located to the south of the present two-story brick Brown Bear Restaurant).

On November 1, 1888, M. K. Cohen announced his intention to run for the position of Justice of the Peace. He failed.

The year, 1889, was more-or-less obliterated from Silverton History. No papers could be found before the November 2 issue of the *Silverton Standard*.

The November 9, paper reported that G. A. Ambold had been found drowned in a spring near his residence in Durango. Ambold founded the Silverton Meat Market in 1875 (Fig. 7). He had been sick for a few days with erysipelas in the face and at times had been delirious. It was presumed that while in this condition, he attempted to get a drink and fell into the spring.

1890 started off with a bang. On January 10, the entire block to the north of Sherwin's stone store and George Hemphill's adjoining boot and shoe store on the east side of Greene Street burned to the ground (Figs. 9 & 10). This was Silverton's worst fire. Hemphill's frame would have burned had not the firemen torn down the frame shack next to his store. The fire started in the old 1875 Centennial or Grand Central Hotel, which had been vacant for more than a year. Probably started by some transient. Ten buildings were completely destroyed. Only four were occupied at the time. R. H. Rohrig was using Breen & McNicholas's old building as a storeroom for beef. The volunteers saved the meat. The old C. S. & N. building, owned by Mr. Newman, was occupied by

Ingersoll & Harris, assayers and engineers. Mrs. Day was renting a small building for a laundry, the other was rented as an office. Everything of value was carried out by the firefighters. Fortunately, there was little wind or the entire north end of town would have probably gone up in smoke. The loss was estimated at $20,000.

In early 1890, J. M. Buzzard, owner of a small fruit, cigar, and tobacco store (located on the northwest corner of 13th and Greene Streets), was appointed. U. S. Postmaster for Silverton. He received permission to move the post office into the Grand Hotel building (present dining room). The move was completed on March 1, 1890. The U. S. Post Office moved out of the Grand on September 25, 1892, to a location a block north. On June 6, 1895, the post office moved to the location that it was to occupy for the next 93 years. The yellow tile brick replaced or covered the original brick front much later. (Fig. 71). (The new 1988 post office is behind the Grand Imperial Hotel on the northeast corner of 12th and Reese Streets).

In early May, two small-time thieves stole a pair of shoes and a vase, which they tried to sell at the Crystal Palace Saloon. They were arrested and sentenced to seventy days in the town jail. It was the practice in early Silverton to use the jail inmates for street repair work. To assure that they would not escape, a large ball and chain was attached to their ankles. After a few days of street work, these two gents took off for the hills, carrying their ball and chain with them, plus the picks and shovels used in the roadwork. The paper stated that it was lucky that the jail was locked or they would have also taken off with the town's blankets.

In late April, 1890, the Malchus Brothers tore down the old frame building, two doors south of the Posey & Wingate brick building. They constructed a building containing two storerooms, one for a rental and the other for their barbershop. During the construction, they noticed that the building occupied by B. W. Thayer, next door to the north, was three inches onto their lot. The building was jacked up and moved over three inches to satisfy the Malchus Brothers.

Silverton turned on electric lights for the first time at six o'clock on the evening of September 20, 1890. They provided electricity only during the evening hours. Of the 435 lights installed, only two did not work.

On November 13, 1890, Silverton pioneer and town founder, Dempsey Reese, died at the age of 56. He was called the father of mining in San Juan County. He had been sick for about a year. Death was caused by pneumonia, contracted about a week prior to his death.

The headquarters of the famed Cow Boy Band (original spelling) of Dodge City, Kansas (Figs. 73 & 74) was moved to Silverton in June, 1890. This band was originally organized and chartered under the laws of Kansas in 1881. The band consisted of ten or twelve cowboy musicians who worked and lived near Dodge City. They were organized to furnish music for stockmen's conventions in Dodge and nearby towns. By 1885, the band contained 20 members. The uniform of the band was the typical attire worn by working cowboys. D. M. Beeson, a well-known musician and cattle owner formed the band. The trademark of the band was the longhorn cattle horns, one purchased by Mr. Beeson in 1878 for $8. This set measured five feet three inches from tip to tip. A second set was presented to the band while playing for the Range Convention in Denver. This set measured seven

Fig. 71. **Then**-1989 photo showing the U. S. Post Office that was used from 1895 until 1988. The west side of Greene Street, between 13th and 14th Streets. (Allan G. Bird photo)

Fig. 72. **Now**-August, 1998 photo of old post office building on Greene Street. (Allan G. Bird photo)

Fig. 73. **Then**-1890. Dodge City Cow Boy Band moved to Silverton that year. The band played for the Washington D. C. inauguration of President Benjamin Harrison. (San Juan Co. Historical Society photo)

Fig. 74. **Then**-July 4, 1891 Dodge City (Silverton) Cow Boy Band. Otto Mears presented the band banner seen in the center of the photo. (San Juan Co. Historical Society photo)

feet and ten inches and was reported to be the largest in the world. It was purchased in South America by a livestock commission firm in Kansas City. The band was the leading attraction during the Washington, D. C. inauguration of President Benjamin Harrison. The reason given for the move to Silverton was the proximity of Silverton to the cattle ranges. Buffalo Bill tried to get the band to go on a worldwide tour, but the men did not want to become full-time musicians, preferring the life of the range. The band was made of 35 well-trained musicians. (Fig. 73 is dated 1890 or early 1891).

William Davies purchased the Fashion Saloon from F. W. Koehler on January 17, 1891. He had the building electrified and held his grand opening in February.

Fig. 75 was taken September 1, 1891. The tall building on the right is Dick's Hall. The new Robins building, across the street from Dick's Hall, was completed in June, 1891. The building contained three businesses. The Uno Clubrooms were on the corner. The St. Charles Restaurant, and Neer & Hanna's Barbershop joined to the south.

B. W. Thayer's building, north of the Malchus Brother's Barbershop, was sold to George Hemphill for $2,500 during the latter part of August. Hemphill had the shoe store that survived the great fire in January, 1890. Hemphill immediately moved into his new store. He occupied the building (Joseph Lacombe's 1876 building next door to the south of the Posey & Wingate brick building) until after the turn of the century.

M. K. Cohen secured the agency for the St. Paul Accident Insurance Company of St. Paul, Minnesota. Never say quit. He also joined the Cow Boy Band as secretary of the organization and base drummer. He soon gave up the insurance business and became associated full-time with the band. While on the road, Cohen posed as the manager of the band. On April 15, 1891, the *Silverton Standard* wrote:

> M. K. Cohen, a former resident of this town, is posing in Denver as the manager of the Dodge City Cow Boy Band. Mr. Cohen is not, never was, and never will be manager of that organization.

In early December, 1891, Cohen committed suicide in Milwaukee. The Milwaukee paper stated that he had been the business manager and part owner of the Cow Boy Band. He was also reported to have been a newspaperman and to have worked for the *San Francisco Chronicle, St. Louis Globe Democrat, New Orleans Picayune, New York World,* and other papers. He apparently was a pathological liar. In January, 1891, Cohen started injecting himself with morphine. He had kept a record of his daily injections. The cause of death was a self-inflicted dose of 1000 grains. He had contemplated suicide before. A "good-bye-world" letter, written in September, was found among his belongings. Clutched in his hand was a scrap of paper on which he had written a prayer in Hebrew characters.

The February 25, 1893, issue of the *Silverton Standard* reported, "Buffalo Bill had purchased the Cow Boy Band and would take it around the world with his Wild West Show."

Fig. 75 is an excellent panoramic view of Silverton taken by the famous photo-

Fig. 75. **Then**-September 1, 1891 panoramic photo by W. H. Jackson. (Colo. Hist. Soc. photo)

Fig. 76. **Now**-March 1990 photo showing approximate scene as Fig. 75. Miner's Union Hospital in foreground occupies space where Snowden's cabin stood. (Allan G. Bird photo)

grapher, William Henry Jackson. The date of the photo is about September 1, 1891. Evidence for the date is as follows: Col. Snowden's cabin, center foreground, has a new peaked roof, which was completed on August 1. The paper raved about the quality of his vegetable garden. By August 1, he had "turnips as large as hens eggs, potatoes, cabbage, lettuce, etc." The garden is clearly visible in the photo. The first snow of the season dusted Kendall Mountain on August 27, 1891. The freshly-painted Robin building (Fig. 75), across the street to the south of the Grand Hotel, was completed in June, 1891.

By 1892, 'old' Silverton was beginning to fade. During the summer of 1892, Mickey Breen replaced the peaked roof of the Sherwin stone building with one that sloped toward the street. He wanted to eliminate shoveling snow that accumulated between his store and the Opera House (old county building). The remainder of the block had been destroyed by fire. On October 1, 1892, the old Senate Saloon was partially destroyed by fire. A new frame building occupied by Corlette & Claque, replaced the Senate by the middle of December. Theodore Dick's large hall burned to the ground December 18, 1892. Fred Helmboldt built the first new brick building (Fig. 77), since the Grand Hotel. It was used as a meat market. This building (now occupied by the Brown Bear Restaurant) was completed in late July, 1893. Helmboldt sold the business, known as the Silverton Meat & Produce Company, to Pearson Brothers. Robert Pearson had opened one of the first meat markets in Silverton in 1876.

Fig. 77. **Now**-1893 Helmboldt building. Occupied by Pearson's Brothers Meat Market from 1893 to 1917. (Allan G. Bird-August, 1998 photo)

1893 was the year of the Great Silver Panic. Many of the mines in the area were forced to close. Silver became so cheap that counterfeiters could make 51 cents on the dollar by faking silver dollars, using the exact silver content of government-issued coins. The barber, C. F. Shulmberg, was afraid the banks would fail. He withdrew his savings and hid them in a trunk. He was robbed of $500 the next day. The Bank of Silverton, organized in 1890, closed temporarily. They reopened in October, initially paying 25 cents on the dollar. The First National Bank weathered the panic. The Denver & Rio Grande Railroad passed into the hands of a receiver. Someone stole the beer from the Silverton Hard Times Club, forcing the members to drink coffee.

Optimism was high by the end of 1893 and things did improve. The real surge in new brick buildings began in 1895. About the end of July, 1894, George Bausman formed a partnership with Mickey Breen in the dry goods business. Two weeks later Breen died, leaving Bausman to run the store. In early March, 1895,

Nathan Shoe Company leased Breen's building (now Pickle Barrel Restaurant). George Bausman moved across the street and built the two-story Bausman building (Figs. 78, 79, 80, 81) in the summer of 1895. Figure 78 shows the building shortly after it was completed in late 1895. The sign protruding from the rear of the building says, "The Standard Bottling Works." (This firm later moved into the building now occupied by the Crewel Elephant on 13th Street). The stores adjacent are: Ed Lussy-Shoes, C. H. H. Kramer-Meats, Wm. Cole-Gent's Furnishings, N. T. Thompson-Second-hand store, and on the right, the post office.

Fig. 78. **Then**-1895 photo of the new Bausman brick building. Looking northwest from 13th and Greene Streets. (Eddie Lorenzon photo)

Knute Benson, who had been in partnership with Eugene McCarthy in the old Star of the West Saloon, had recently been working in the Hub Saloon. In early May, 1895, Benson took over Jane Bowen's old Westminster Hall on the corner. Jane and William Bowen had sold the Westminster to Charles Jones and Morris Lonergan on April 1, 1889. William Bowen died on June 22, 1891. Benson owned the rich Butterfly-Terrible Mines near Ophir (which he sold for $200,000 in 1899). He soon began to buy property adjacent to his new corner saloon. In July, Jones & Lonegran completed their new brick saloon (Fig. 83, on the southeast corner of 12th and Greene Streets).

On May 11, 1895, the contract was let for the new brick county building (Fig. 82 on the northwest corner of 13th and Reese Streets).

Lloyd and Stanger began building their new false-front Silver Dollar Saloon (Fig. 83, on the lot previously occupied by the burned-out Dick's Hall, next to the livery). In late February, 1898, Grant Cardwell and Walter Fowler got into a scrap in which Fowler came out the loser. Both men had been drinking heavily. At 11

Fig. 79. **Then**-1954 photo of the Bausman brick building. Looking northwest from 13th and Greene Streets. For years, the building served as a drug store. (Ruth Gregory photo)

Fig. 80. **Recent**-March, 1990 photo showing the Bausman building and Lode Theater. The Cole-Hoffman building and the old post office on the far right. The theater is now an art studio. (Allan G. Bird photo)

Fig. 81. **Now**-August, 1998 photo of the Bausman building. (Allan G. Bird photo)

Fig. 82. **Now**-January, 1999 photo of the 1895 county building, located on the northwest corner of 14th and Reese Streets. (Allan G. Bird photo)

Fig. 83. **Then**-Photo c.a. 1900 showing Jones & Lonergan's Saloon on left and Lloyd & Stanger's Silver Dollar Saloon 2nd from right, next to the Patterson Brother's Livery. (Patty Dailey photo)

Fig. 84. **Now**-January, 1999 photo of the buildings now occupying the sites of Jones & Lonergan's Saloon (far left) and Lloyd & Stanger's Silver Dollar Saloon (the two-story building next to the brick livery on the right). (Allan G. Bird photo)

o'clock in the evening, Cardwell entered Billy Stanger's Silver Dollar Saloon. He encountered Fowler and a group of his friends drinking. Cardwell drew his gun and shot Fowler in the leg, shattering the ankle. Cardwell was arrested and placed in jail on $600 bond. Fowler was taken to Durango. His leg became progressively worse and amputation was required. A few days later, Fowler died. Shortly after his arrest, Cardwell escaped from jail. He left a note saying that he would return when he could raise enough money for a fair trial. He was never captured and he never returned. William Stanger sold out all interest in his Silver Dollar Saloon in late August, 1899. He retired to California.

Charles Fischer, who owned the Silverton Brewing Company, tore down the old Arion Saloon and Robert Robert's Bowling Alley. He constructed the two-story brick Teller House building. The building was completed in June, 1896 (Figs. 85 & 86). Two saloons opened in the rooms now occupied by the French Bakery Restaurant. The Landry Brothers operated the Frog Saloon and the Todeschi Brother's the French Boys Saloon.

Fig. 85. **Then**-1905 photo showing the Teller House. (Fritz Klinke photo)

Fig. 86. **Now**-Teller House in Mar., 1997. (Allan Bird photo)

A rather interesting story evolved around the Teller House about the turn of the century. About 1970, Mr. & Mrs. George Bingle were bottle hunting on Hazelton Mountain, northeast of Silverton, when they dug up a rather large can near an old miner's cabin. Inside of the can was another can. Upon opening the inner can, they found all the personal papers, even postage stamps, of the previous occupant of the cabin. Included in the artifacts were several letters written to the owner, Anton Linquist, between 1900 and 1902, by the wife of the owner of the Teller House, Madaline Bettray.

Anton Lindquist was a blacksmith by trade, who came to this country from Sweden in 1885. He arrived in the San Juans in 1895. He worked at the nearby mines during the summer months to earn enough money to work on his own prospect on Hazelton Mountain during the winter. He frequently came to town and stayed at the Teller House. During his stays, he developed a romance with the owner's wife. They would pass secret notes to each other. Her notes always ended with "burn this, this is the worst." Unfortunately, he cherished each note and kept it in his private "can."

Anton had no use for the miner's unions and frequently worked as a "scab" during labor strikes. He had admission cards from the Smuggler Union Mine at Telluride, and the Independence Mine at Cripple Creek, allowing him to pass through the armed guards protecting the mines during strikes. He became hated in Silverton and, in one of the few letters that he wrote home, that he never mailed, he told of a mob of men approaching his cabin one dark night. He hid in the timber and escaped their wrath but was forced to return to Minnesota where he had relatives. He stated that four men followed him all the way to Minnesota, but he was able to elude them and returned to Colorado Springs, where he worked in a coal mine for a while. After the strikes were over and things cooled down, he returned to Silverton and began his affair with Madaline.

His first letter to her was about his loaning Joe Terry, manager of the Sunnyside Mine, $300. Terry was having trouble making ends meet at the mine but he did eventually pay Lindquist back in small installments. His letter to Madaline read:

> I talked to Joe Terry and he told me to inquire to J. H. Terry (Joe's father), Eureka, for to receive the money that is due to me and in these circumstances I follow his advice because I am not with good health and am unable to work at present.

Both Anton's and Madaline's use of the English language left much to be desired. In his can was a well-used Swedish-English dictionary. Madaline answered:

Dear Anton:

> No dear I have good lungs only I took a bad cold and they feel raw and sore. Can't hardly speak. I know you wish well, I can read it in your face—You don't feel like you can idle any time away because you want

want to get so far with your mine that you can take out proceeds after you are so far, then you will be contented and you have my whole soul and wish, for you deserve it, and need it. Only go slow and easy for we all will come to it earlier that way. Make yourself just at home, and don't work, take it all easy—always keep all your money, never let no one have one cent—for it is always trouble to get it back—it is easy to give but hard to get back—this losing time and running after people is not a pleasant thing so that will give you one good lesson love—let them all look out for themselves. Well I can't tell nothing of myself only what you already know, so I will rest a little now for they all will come in about 11 or 12 to 5 in the morning. Write to me anytime you like for I love to read your mind. Excuse my scribbling and hurry. I was sorry I had to give John McIntosh your bed in No. 9 as he wants to stay till he gets his money, maybe a week, always takes cot in No. 9 Bye bye love.

Madaline

Unfortunately, we have only copies of her letters, with the exception of one that he did not send to her. These letters give a feeling of the hardships that the early settlers of Silverton endured and an insight into their dreary lives. He must have written her complaining of his health problems as her next letters are as follows:

Dear Anton:

I am awful sorry to hear your legs are sore and tired and that you had to walk so far yesterday in the snow for walking now is hard and I don't want you to do too much of it, although it is nice to see your face and see you at home, for this is your home as long as it is mine. Work is well if some pleasure is mixed with it, so let us be happy as long as we can live in hope. As far as understanding, it is a pleasure for me when you make me study, never mind me teaching you. You are cute enough. I admit that my eyes express themselves sometime, and you are just cute enough to read them. They say still water runs deep and you can see that I am a good scholar. But remember that I will puzzle you many times yet. You didn't guess right last night. All the same, you can write me a few lines, as I love to read it. It makes me think well. I hope we will understand each other some day. Your eyes speak for your heart tonight.

Madaline

Dear Anton:

I hope you will forgive me for letting you wait so long. I understood the last time when you were here that you were not going up that day until I got up? Then I found out that you went up. I will give you room 16 so you can answer this before you leave. Well dear, how can I speak more freely, only to wait on and sometime we will git a chance. We will always be one until the time comes when we can be free about it. As long as there is life there are chances if we will be quiet and have our passion. We will gain by this. Just so I can see you I will be pleased. Whenever I see you it is just like sunshine in my life. I can't help it. My feeling act for itself, so love answer. I will be passion until I read your dear notes. Only excuse my bad scribbling as I have to be always in a hurry. Good night my love, pleasant dreams until—well you know.

Madaline

Darling:

He had to give up his bed in the office to that sick boy and he will stay with me tonight so dear we have to call it off tonight till some other time. The house is crowded, we had to let three go away. The storm brings them down. Well good night love. Tear this note up—Will see you tomorrow before you leave.

Madaline

Hello Dear:

I saw you love, when you came. I thought of you last night that is why you came down. I was glad when I seen you. When will you go away? You can take No. 7, the same bed. I will see you sometime. Don't go up in that storm, wait until it is settled for it is dangerous now with the drifting. Well, do write me a few lines, tell me all what you have to say.

Madaline

Dear:

As I could not sleep one moment last night you will not blame me for these few lines as them few lines you wrote on the little slip meant lots. They set me a studying. Don't get discouraged about work for we all have to work. Work is what keeps our minds occupied and the old saying is that work makes life sweet. I work for I like work. I made myself a new dress and my girl one also. I tend to all kinds of business, up all hours of the night, for it seems like I have to tend to it all. It is as hard as to work with pick and shovel. Hardly no outdoor air at all.

Last night my brother came in. He is in the stock business and it took four hours of work for me for I have some stock with him. He lives in Grand Junction. Everything hangs on me just now for it seems all comes to me. All the boys in the house come to me to do this or that and I have to please all or talk to all in order to do justice to business. So we know that there is better days coming and may not have to do so much. Live for our pleasure, so if you don't weary I won't, and we will do our best. I will hand this to you tomorrow morning when you go away and think of you till I will see you again. We can't live unless we do something. I will try and get a few moments rest. Take the best care of yourself so nothing happens to you. Don't get in no slide or don't slip and fall. Go slow and take you time for you have something to live for. I will close, it is 4 o'clock in the morning. Just as soon as the weather gets warm, I will take a walk every once in a while to your place. First Mr. B (her husband) and I will go with you one day until I see the trail, then I will walk to it myself for to get outdoor exercise and fresh air. No one will know where I go. He can easily take care of the business daytime. Answer this question particularly so I will know your opinion about it. Today is the first of December and March and April will be here soon. He will go east in May and stay 8 weeks. Well dear, never keep these letters, as soon as you read them burn them up for we don't want no one to know our business, for it is best. Unknowing facts is the winner-so please.

Madaline

The last letter we have is from Anton to Madaline; one that was never delivered.

My Adorable Love:

I will hereby certify to you that I love you next of God but I have to work against myself to keep my passion invisible. My dear girl, I will gladly follow your statement. I will wait the time. It is sufficient to my heart that you are my love. I hope we will have the pleasure side by side my dear girl. How are you tonight? You look well. If you get sick I get sick too. If not to the body but to the feelings and I catch it just the same.

Anton

Sadly, their love was never fulfilled. In 1905, Mr. Bettray sold the Teller House and moved to Denver to open a pie factory on south Broadway at a cost of $11,000. He spent $40,000 on a home and business. The last letter that Anton received from his relatives in Sweden was dated 1909. Included in his papers were numerous ads for patent medicine cures for syphilis and gonorrhea. Madaline may have gotten more than she bargained for. He buried his letters and personal papers and never returned.

Fig. 87. **Recent**-Anton Linquist's cabin in 1975. (Allan G. Bird photo)

The May 2, 1896 issue of the *Silverton Standard* quoted the *Durango Wage Earner's* article:

> Silverton has more new buildings in the course of erection than any other town in the San Juan. She has more gold and silver lying around in the side of her mountains than the world could coin into money in two or three generations. There are no flies on Silverton.

The large stone building (Fig. 88), now occupied by a clothing shop on 13th Street, was built in 1896 as the San Juan Livery Company's stable. It remained a livery stable until June, 1907 when Pete Orella opened his Standard Bottling Works.

Fig. 88. **Then**-c.a. 1907 photo of the old San Juan Livery Stables. It became the Standard Bottling Works in 1907. (Jim Bell photo)

Fig. 89. **Now**-May, 1999 photo of the above building. (Allan G. Bird photo)

In June, 1896, John Lorenzon and Joe Grivette tore down C. F. Schulmberg's old barber shop that burned in late December, 1895. They built the Chicago Saloon (Fig. 90). The building, with its bay window, serves today as a gift shop.

Fig. 90. **Then**-c.a.1897 photo of the Chicago Saloon. (Jim Bell photo)

Fig. 91. **Now**-May, 1999 photo of the old Chicago Saloon. (Allan G. Bird photo)

The old Metropolitan Saloon, known as the Blue Front, installed a rifle range for the entertainment of their heavy drinkers.

The old Senate Saloon, originally Goode's Saloon, lately operated by Corlette & Claque, was now the Germania Beer Hall under the management of Henry Breining. This saloon was later named the Arcade, not to be confused with the present Arcade on Blair Street.

The Doud Brothers now owned the Exchange Livery. Early one spring morning, a small boy came to Merrill Doud and offered to sell him an empty whiskey bottle. Doud informed the small one that he only bought bottles if they were full of whiskey and offered ten cents if he returned with it full. The urchin left and soon returned with a full bottle. Doud happily paid the boy his ten cents. That night, as Doud was leaving his favorite saloon, the bartender stopped him, reminding him, "that some small boy had come in earlier, saying you wanted your whisky bottle filled. I charged the 50 cents to your tab."

Joe Satore had operated the saloon, north of the Teller House, for the past year, Louis Giacomelli purchased half interest in the business in April, 1897. A short time later, Giacomelli bought out Satore. In 1897, Giacomelli had a photograph taken of his new business (Fig. 92). Standing to the right of his dad, on the barrel, is Fiore Giacomelli, age 3. When Fiore was about 4 or 5 years old, he and his sister were watching their mother cut the heads off of some chickens. After the mother had left, the sister suggested that Fiore put his hand on the chopping block and they would play "chicken." Not knowing any better, he did and she chopped his index finger off. It was not until she was on her deathbed many years later that she admitted to the act. Fiore's older brother had caught the blame all those years. Fiore died in 1989 at the age of 96.

Fig. 92. **Then**-1897 photo of Louis Giacomelli in apron with his 3-year-old son next to him. Old Turf Exchange Saloon. building was crushed by snow in April, 1914. Now a leather shop next door to the north of the Teller House. (Fiore Giacomelli photo)

Louis Giacomelli remained in this building until July 1899, when he and his new partner, Matt Chiono, moved into the old county building next door to the present Pickle Barrel Restaurant.

In April, 1900, Chiono & Giacomelli moved next door into the old stone Sherwin building. They opened the Iron Mountain Saloon. (The sign can still be seen on the side of the building). This establishment operated until 1916, when state Prohibition closed the saloons. In 1916, it became a recreation hall offering pool, billiards, soft drinks and a soda fountain. After the death of Louis, his son, Fiori and his wife, Maggie, operated the business throughout the Depression, moving it across the street to the Posey & Wingate building in the 1940's. Fig. 93 shows Louis Giacomelli and his wife standing beside their new automobile. The word, saloon, has been painted over with black paint. This dates the photo as after January, 1916. Years of weathering have exposed the original saloon sign (Fig. 94.)

Fig. 93. **Then**-c.a. 1916 photo of Louis Giacomelli and his wife with their new car in front of the old Iron Mountain Saloon. Note word, Saloon, has been blacked out. (Fiore Giacomelli photo)

Fig. 94. **Now**-May, 1999 photo of the Iron Mountain Saloon sign. The word Saloon has been exposed by years of weathering. (Allan G. Bird photo)

In March, 1897, Bowman and Melton let the contract for the construction of the "Big Brick Barn" livery stable (Fig. 95) on the east side of Greene Street between 11th and 12th Streets. This building contained Silverton's first elevator, capable of lifting 1,500 pounds. Horses were kept upstairs and the wagons on the main floor. Melton bought out Bowman in 1901. Clint Bowman moved to Denver to form the Merchant's Biscuit Company, later to become the National Biscuit Company. Bowman and his father had worked in the kitchen of the Gold King Mine at Gladstone. Clint's father made soda crackers for the men and they were such a hit that Clint decided to share the recipe with the world.

The Patterson Brothers purchased the livery in July, 1906 (Fig. 96). After the arrival of the automobile, it became Silverton's first garage. Today it is occupied by a gift shop.

Fig. 95. **Then**-c.a. 1900. Bowman & Melton's "Big Brick Barn" Livery Stable. (Patty Dailey photo)

Fig. 96. **Then**-1906. New Patterson Bros. sign on the livery building. (Eddie Lorenzon photo)

Fig. 97. **Now**-August 1998 photo of "Big Brick Barn" Livery Stable. (Allan G. Bird photo)

In October 1897, George Lacy purchased for $8,200 the building built by Tom Blair in 1883 and the adjoining "new" 1884 St. Julien Restaurant building, occupied by two saloons run by Henry Sherman and Larson & Berquist. Lafayette Henry and Tom Allen opened the new Senate Saloon in the northernmost building on November 21, 1899 (Fig. 98). Lafe Henry obtained complete control of the Senate in 1900. He died on May 20, 1901, at the age of 50. Henry had 13 children, three of whom preceded him in death, the oldest being 21 and the youngest six weeks. His widow ran the saloon for a short time before selling it to Berquist and Johnson. They retained the Senate Saloon name. These buildings remain today.

Fig. 98. **Then**-1900. "New" Senate Saloon. Owner Lafe Henry in white apron. Henry died in 1901. "Old" Senate Saloon was on the southeast corner of 13th and Greene Streets. (San Juan Co. Hist. Society photo)

Pearce & Reynolds replaced their old Ten Pin Alley with a new one-story brick building, which opened on July 1, 1898 (Fig. 99). The old English Kitchen, next door to the north of Pierce & Reynolds, was torn down. A new brick building was constructed (Fig. 99) and reopened as the English Kitchen. Billy Stanger later bought the building and opened a saloon. The roof and front of this building was crushed by snow in the 1970's and only the walls remain.

By the end of 1898, half of the block along the east side of Greene Street south of 12th Street was occupied by new buildings.

Fig. 99. **Then**-c.a. 1900. Reynold's & Pierces Saloon on the right and the English Kitchen on the left. Both were built in 1898. (Patty Dailey photo)

Fig. 100. **Now**-January, 1999 photo of the two structures occupying the site of the English Kitchen on the left, and Reynold's and Pierce's Saloon, on the right. (Allan G. Bird photo)

In early November, 1899, John Perrung left Silverton for good. He had opened his New York Bakery in 1883. His building was soon to be occupied by the Silverton Supply Company as a grocery and supply store (Fig. 101). Years later, Fiore Giacomelli's brother, Louis, opened the Best Cafe in this building. The author was forced to eat many a meal in this restaurant in 1959 while on a geological mine mapping project. I coined the phrase that, "The Best is none too good." The building was crushed by snow in the early 1980's and was replaced by the two-story frame building, now occupied by the Silverton Minerals and Gift Shop.

Fig. 101. **Then**-1901 photo showing the Silverton Supply Company Store on the far right. (Eddie Lorenzon photo)

Fig. 102. **Then**-1952 photo of heavy snow. Old Silverton Supply Store is in the center, above the rear of the car. It was the Best Cafe at this time. (Jim Bell photo)

Fig. 103. **Now**-May, 1999 photo showing the site of the old Silverton Supply Store. This building was built in 1983. It is the only new building on the block. (Allan G. Bird photo)

The Hub Saloon, in the Grand Hotel Building, made headlines in late April, 1900. It seems that Jack "Ten Day" Turner had become enamored with one of Blair Street's fallen angels by the name of Blanche. He heard that Blanche was having a drink with Jack Lambert in the Hub. Enraged at the thought, he entered the saloon and saw the couple drinking at the bar. Without saying a word, he pulled his gun and began firing at Lambert and Blanche. He got off five shots, two of which hit Lambert in the right side, about two inches below the arm. The bullets caused only flesh wounds. The editor of the *Standard* happened to be in the saloon at the time and reported the following:

> 'Johnnie Dettines was riveted to the spot, until after the third shot, when he made two jumps and landed in the wine room without a scratch.'
> 'Herman Strobel tried to climb the water pipe line.'
> 'King, the barber, after listening to the sweet song of the first bullet, took a header under the faro layout.'
> 'Joe fainted dead away and in that condition pulled a card table over on top of himself.'
> Ross ducked.'
> 'A big Swede crawled under the wine room door and went through the alley window.'
> 'The editor of this paper, who was on the spot for the express purpose of chronicling the item, never moved from his seat but was cool and collected throughout the whole affair, notwithstanding other

assertions to the contrary.'

Jack Lambert's wife divorced him over the incident. "Ten Day" was sent to Canon City for a few years' rest.

Ground was broken during the week ending June 9, 1900, for the new Miner's Union building, now the American Legion Hall (Fig. 104). The new building was a large two-story brick structure that for many years housed H. G. Prosser's Furniture and Undertaking establishment. The furniture rooms were in the front and the undertaking parlor in the rear of the building.

Fig. 104. **Then**-Miner's Union building. Ground was broken for the building in early June, 1900. Southwest corner of 11th and Greene Streets. Prosser's Furniture Store signs on awnings. Undertaking rooms at rear. (Jim Bell photo)

Fig. 105. **Now**-August, 1998 photo of old Miner's Union Building. Now the American Legion Hall on ground floor and the local San Juan Theater Group upstairs. The upstairs was recently restored for theater use. (Allan G. Bird photo)

During the last week of December, 1890, Earnest Hoffman purchased the old Silverton Hotel, changing the name to the Hoffman House. His son, Earnest Jr., told the writer that his dad "lost his butt in that hotel. The miners would spend their money on whiskey and women and never pay their board bills."

Knute Benson began tearing down the four buildings, which had contained the old Westminster Hall, a Chinese laundry, Stahlnecker's Steam Laundry, and the old Metropolitan Saloon, recently renamed the Blue Front. Benson built the large two-story Benson building (Fig. 107) over the four lots (Fig. 106). The County Club Saloon was located on the corner and was operated by "Kid" Whitelaw and "Billy" Koehler. The sign still decorates the top corner of the building. The Benson building cost $35,000 to build.

Fig. 106. **Then**-1895 photo showing the four buildings on the right that were demolished in 1900 to make way for the large brick Benson building. (Ruth Gregory photo)

Fig. 107. **Now**-August, 1998 photo showing the 1901 Benson building on the right. (Allan G. Bird photo)

"Billy" Cole and Fritz Hoffman began construction of the large Cole-Hoffman building in 1900. Cole and Hoffman were close friends. Hoffman built his second-hand and furniture store before Cole. He moved in on July 25, 1901. Cole's brickwork was completed on September 28, 1901. They designed the building with a common wall that would separate them. The double building cost $27,000 to build.

About mid-August, 1901, J. N. Anderson began construction of the two-story brick building (just south of the present Town Hall) (Figs. 108 & 109). This building was used as an undertaking parlor, a clothing store, millinery shop and, for many years, by the Silverton Telephone Company. Today it is a gift shop.

Fig. 108. **Then**-July 4, 1904 photo showing the Anderson building on the left and Wyman building on the right. Also, the Iron Mountain Saloon and the Germania Beer Hall. Note the wooden sidewalks. (Eddie Lorenzon photo)

Fig. 109. **Now**-March, 1990 photo of the Anderson building. (Allan G. Bird photo)

On the southwest corner of 14th and Greene Streets, Louis Wyman began excavation on October 12, 1901, for the two-story red-sandstone building (Figs. 110 & 111), known today as the Wyman Hotel. Wyman was an old-timer in Silverton. He opened the Silverton Restaurant in 1881, located a few doors south of the present Wyman building. About a year later, he gave up the restaurant business and moved to Ophir. Wyman returned a short time later and became prosperous in the packing and freighting business. Louis Wyman dedicated his new building to the mule. He personally cut the stone bas-relief of the mule (Fig. 111), now visible on the corner of the roof.

Fig. 110. **Now**-August, 1998 photo of the Wyman building, now the Wyman Hotel, completed in 1902. (Allan G. Bird photo)

Fig. 111. **Now**-Mule carved by Louis Wyman for his 1902 Wyman buiilding. (Allan G. Bird photo)

+ CHAPTER 3 +

SILVERTON-THEN AND NOW   1902-1921 and Beyond

The February 8, 1902, paper announced that Knute Benson had died in California from an operation. His funeral was held in the lobby of the Benson building. His was one of the largest funerals ever seen in Silverton. He was born in Sweden and was past 63 years of age at the time of his death.

The two Lacy buildings (Fig. 58), occupied by Henry Sherman and Berquist & Johnson, both saloons, were sold for $14,000. They were purchased by Lacy a few years earlier for $8,200.

The old Masonic Hall (San Juan Herald) building (Fig. 112) on the corner of 13th and Reese Streets, was reported in the papers as being torn down and a new building (Fig. 113) constructed during the summer of 1902. A quick comparison of the before and after photos shows that the old building was not torn down but enlarged by an addition.

Mrs. Hughes, proprietress of the Alma House, (Fig 114) built the present stone structure (midway between Blair and Mineral Streets on the North Side of 10th Street) in the spring of 1902. The original Alma House was a wooden structure, which was destroyed by fire.

The new county jail was completed in early August, 1902. This jail now houses the San Juan County Historical Society Museum.

The contract for the new municipal electric light plant was let for $1,230 (Fig. 115) in late July, 1902. The total cost for the entire plant was $30,000. It was located on 11th Street east of Cement Street toward the river. The structure was built in the middle of the street.

Hotel Melton was the name given to the new hotel in the Benson building.

The Wyman building, started in 1901, was completed in mid-November, 1902, at a cost of $30,000.

The Bank of Silverton (located in the corner building of the Grand Hotel) was closed on January 2, 1903. J. H. Robins, president of the bank, disappeared. A reward was offered for information on his whereabouts. A few days later, his body was found under a water tank along the railroad tracks. He had shot himself in the head. An examination of the books revealed that he had embezzled large amounts of money from the bank. The *San Juan Prospector* offered a crumb of comfort to the *Silverton Standard,* who lost $2,000 in the bank failure, with the statement: "What was a newspaper man doing with $2,000 anyhow? He ought to lose it."

On January 12, 1903, George Bausman, the owner of the Bausman building, died from appendicitis. He left a wife and eleven children. Several of his descendants live in Silverton today (1999). His wife and son operated the business for a year. On June 6, 1904, the building was leased to Sam Wittrow, who opened his Famous Dry Goods Store. Wittrow continued in business for 17 years, leaving during the depression of 1921 (Fig. 116). The building was occupied by a series of drug stores until 1982. Since then it has been used for a variety of tourist-related businesses.

Fig. 112. **Then**-San Juan Herald building, now the Masonic building. Photo taken September 20, 1883, at 1 o'clock in the afternoon. Southwest corner of 13th and Reese Streets. (San Juan Co. Hist. Soc. photo)

Fig. 113. **Now**-March, 1990 photo of the old San Juan Herald building. Note the new addition added above the left door and at the end of the right tall windows. Last upper window had been changed. Now the Masonic building. (Allan G. Bird photo)

Fig. 114. **Now**-May, 1999 photo of Mrs. Hughes's 1902 Alma House. Now a bed and breakfast hotel. (Allan G. Bird photo)

Fig. 115. **Then**-1902 Municipal Light Plant. 11th Street, east of Cement Street. (San Juan Co. Hist. Soc. photo)

Fig. 116. **Then**-Labor Day, 1908 parade. Sam Wittrow's "Famous" Dry Goods store on the right with awning. Koehler's Saloon on left. From 1952 until Sept. 30, 1998, Koehler's building was occupied by the *Silverton Standard* newspaper. Posey & Wingate building in the center. (Jim Bell photo)

Ground was broken for the new Catholic church (Fig. 117) about mid-July, 1906. The church was dedicated on April 27, 1907.

Fig. 117. **Now**-1907 Catholic church. (Allan G. Bird-January, 1999 photo)

Bert Brown, the butcher, tore down the old frame next to the Grand Hotel and built a one-story stone-front rental building (now occupied by the Parlor Gift Shop). The building was completed and occupied by S. D. Cunningham, the druggist, October 1, 1903 (Fig. 118). Cunningham's Drug Store had been located in the Grand Hotel for several years. (Except for the present Silverton Minerals and Gift Shop, the block containing the Grand Imperial Hotel appears as it did in late 1903.)

Fig. 118. **Now**-Bert Brown's 1903 building. Occupied by Cunningham's Drug Store until 1920. Cunningham sold to the Rexall Pharmacy Co. Next door to the Grand Imperial Hotel. Now a gift shop. (Allan G. Bird 1989 photo)

On October 1, 1903, Hemphill & McCrimmon's Shoe and Dry Goods Store moved from the building (located next door to the south of the Posey & Wingate brick building,) to the Wyman building. Hemphill bought a lottery-type ticket and won a ranch on the Uintah Indian Reservation in Utah. He retired to his new ranch in May, 1906. McCrimmon continued the business.

Crebles moved his jewelry store into the Hemphill's old store and operated for a few years. At age 90, he moved to a building across the street from the post office, where he operated until his death at age 93. After Grebles left, a pool hall, fruit, and confectionery store was established by J. Papadakis & Company.

In 1905, F. W. Koehler moved into the Hemphill's old building with a saloon called "Koehlers" (Fig. 116). The *Silverton Standard and the Miner,* moved in about 1952. The *Standard* is the oldest continuously operated newspaper in western Colorado. On September 30, 1998, the paper moved into the new 1998 building built by Brent Westlund on the site of the old Bordeleau Hardware Co. (Fig. 65).

Excavation for the foundation of the Avon Hotel (Fig. 119), known then as the Sherwood building, began in April, 1904. F. 0. Sherwood operated a meat market in the old wooden store next to the new building. The building was completed in December, 1904, at a cost of $ 10,000.

Fig. 119. **Then**-1938 fire that gutted the Sherwood building (Avon Hotel). The hotel was immediately rebuilt. Northwest corner of 10th and Blair (Empire) Streets. (Tom Savich photo)

Fig. 120. **Now**-May, 1999 photo of Avon Hotel. (Allan G. Bird photo)

For years, no one knew the combination to the safe in the Hub Saloon. The owners kept this little secret to themselves. During the summer of 1903, someone inadvertently locked the safe, For days they tried to open it, even bringing in a professional safecracker. They finally had to send to Denver to find someone who could do the job. On September 3, 1904, a masked-man entered the Hub Saloon, a little before one o'clock in the morning. Herman Stroble was in charge of the bar

Page 112

during Jack Slatterly's, the owner's, absence. The man, with guns drawn, ordered everyone to throw up their hands. Stroble, being only a few feet from the bandit, decided to try and stop the robbery. He jumped for the man, who began firing. Two slugs hit Stroble, one in the breast and one in the leg. He continued to struggle and succeeded in forcing the release of one weapon after four shots had been fired. Weakened by his wounds, Stroble staggered out the front door and fell to the ground. He was quickly picked up by some men passing by and taken to the lobby of the hotel, where his wounds were dressed. He eventually recovered.

The highwayman, who saw the growing crowd outside, knew that his plan had been foiled. He ran for the back and made a hasty exit through a closet window into the alley.

One of the four shots fired at Stroble went wide and hit John Loftus, a miner who was sitting at the bar. The shot inflicted a mortal wound on Loftus. His last words were: "My God, I'm done for." The other bullet passed through the arm of James Bothwell, the bartender, imbedding itself in the bar. His wounds were minor. Sheriff Casad arrived shortly after the man had escaped. They searched for him throughout the night. At seven o'clock the next morning, they found the body of the robber in the alley between Reese and Snowden Streets, near 14th Street. He had shot himself in the mouth with his .44-caliber Colt.

The Chinese were driven out of Silverton in 1902. The void created by the exit of the Chinese was quickly filled by an influx of black families. They took over as porters and clean-up men in the saloons. The black population, about 25-30 people, raised enough money to purchase the old wooden Catholic church in 1905. They moved the building to a lot on Mineral Street (Fig. 121). It was dedicated as the African Methodist-Episcopal Church.

Fig. 121. **Then**-1914 photo showing the African Methodist-Episcopal church building in the foreground. Between 12th and 13th Streets, on Mineral Street. (Eddie Lorenzon photo)

Prejudice against the Chinese came to a head on Blair Street in 1902. For years, the Chinese operated laundries and restaurants in Silverton. The newspapers of the day always attached the descriptive adjectives of, "pig-tailed, almond-eyed celestials" or similar derogatory terms when writing of the Chinese. For the most part, the Chinese were extremely hard-working, industrious people. Because of their religious beliefs, they were referred to as heathens. The introduction of opium joints to Silverton was their main drawback. Many of the women on Blair Street took to the "pipe" to relieve their dreary existence.

About the turn of the century, after the formation of the labor unions, agitation against the Chinese increased to the level of violence. On February 8, 1902, the unions published a hate letter in the *Silverton Standard* that read as follows:

Appeal to the People

Do you want the yellow man or the white man? We, as organized labor, ask the people of Silverton and San Juan County for their full support in regards to the Chinese question, which is a serious question to be considered.

As citizens they are a failure; they do not assimilate as citizens and their habits are so obnoxious that they become the most undesirable class of people in the community in which they reside. The opium habit, which has destroyed thousands of lives, is ready to destroy more if not checked. The Chinese dens in this city have destroyed over three hundred human beings. How long are you going to stand for this? Is it not time to do something while the evil is yet in its infancy?

No white man can compete with their labor on account of their cheapness in living. Who reaps the benefit from them? The butcher and grocer may at present, but let them increase and where are you? Look at San Francisco, California, and Portland, Oregon. Beware! This is a warning for the future. Why not be men and act as such? Look at Cripple Creek, Leadville and Colorado Springs. Why don't they have Chinese? Are we not the same kind of men, or are we weaklings? If it were not for the powers of the world, where would the white people who are in China be today? Stop and consider this vital question. Do you want them? If not, then join us.

As we intend, THEY MUST GO.

Executive Committee
W. F. & M. No. 26
Cooks and Waiters Union 16.
Federal Labor Union 112

Whereas, the Chinese are a public nuisance and a detriment to the public welfare; and

Whereas, the white laborer cannot compete with the Chinese labor; therefore, be it

Resolved, that we, the Silverton Miner's Union No. 26, W. F. M., do hereby declare a boycott on all Chinese; and be it further

Resolved, that we ask all union men and fair-mined citizens to withdraw their patronage from all Chinamen.

All but a few of the Chinese packed up and left for Durango or Ouray. Several had built businesses that had been in operation for years. One man, by the name of W. S. Hung, owned a small wooden shack located on the east side of Blair Street about midway between 11th and 12th Streets. He opened his small laundry in 1894, which became known as "Spider's." He did much of the laundry for the "Soiled Doves" of Blair Street and was well accepted until the unions bullied the population into following their boycott. On the night of May 12, 1902, a mob of angry whites decided to drive the last Chinaman out of Silverton. As the mob approached W. S. Hung's small home and laundry, he panicked and fired two shots through the door in an effort to stop them from entering. The mob returned the fire with three shots. The paper's comment that, "This Chinaman did not accompany the crowd," would indicate that they had murdered him. This was not the case. Terrified, he was taken with the remaining Chinese. Ropes were placed around their necks and they were marched to the edge of town and told to follow the railroad tracks to Durango. One or two of them, who were well liked in the past, persuaded their captors to let them return and sell their property and retain their possessions.

The new Silverton National Bank was formed to 1905, locating in the Ballou brick building (next door to the south of the Robin building).

Dr. Pasco built a new frame opera house near the middle of the block south of the Miner's Union building (American Legion Hall). The first week's attraction by the Hanler Comedy Company was described as "simply awful."

The Oxford Beer Depot was opened in the old "Fashion" building in 1905.

The wooden Exchange Livery was replaced in 1906 by a two-story brick structure, covering the space occupied by the wooden livery and the Hesperus Coal building (Fig. 122).

Fig.122. **Then**-July 4, 1905 photo showing the old Exchange Livery and Hesperus Coal Company. Both buildings were torn down in 1906 and the new two-story brick livery completed in 1907. The Teller House is on the left and the old Fashion Saloon on the right, It was the Oxford Beer Depot in 1905. (Fritz Klinke photo)

Fig. 123. **Then**-Sept. 5, 1910 photo. Labor Day parade showing the new two-story brick Exchange Livery (above stagecoach) completed Sept. 1, 1906. Writing on the photo says, "Mrs. Cotton-first woman-Frank Harwood-First boy born in Silverton." Frank Harwood died on September 19, 1906. Photo was mislabeled. (Colorado Historical Society photo)

Fig. 124. **Now**-August, 1998 photo of the Exchange Livery in the center. The second story was removed sometime after 1932. Now a gift shop. The building on the right replaced the old Fashion Saloon building. The 1896 Teller House is on the left. (Allan G. Bird photo)

During the construction of their new building (Figs 121 & 122), the Doud Brothers occupied the old San Juan Livery, later the Standard Bottling Works. They moved into the new two-story brick building on September 1, 1906. The new livery cost $20,000 to build.

The young telegraph operator at the railroad depot had his hand crushed by the keystone used in the construction of the arched doorway of the livery building. He was helping to unload it from the train.

The second story of the brick building was removed sometime after 1932.

The old French Boy's Saloon in the Teller House, next door to the Livery, was now the Office Saloon.

Excavation for the basement of the new San Juan County Courthouse began on August 10, 1906 and the foundation was completed on November 2. Construction was halted until the spring of 1907. The building was completed in late December, 1907 (Figs. 125 & 126).

Fig. 125. **Then**-Photo of the 1907 San Juan County Court House shortly after completion. 1902 Jail is to the right of the building. (Eddie Lorenzon photo)

Fig. 126. **Now**-January, 1999 photo of the court house. (Allan G. Bird photo)

On September 19, 1906, Frank Harwood, the first boy born in Silverton on December 5, 1875, died of pneumonia at the age of 30. He had been working as the electrician in charge of the power plant at the Silver Lake Mine.

Col. F. M. Snowden left Silverton for the last time in late May, 1907. His parting tribute by the May 25, 1907, *Silverton Standard* was as follows:

> No crankier individual than old man Snowden ever existed, yet despite that crankiness, the soul of honor invariably cropped out. Made enough, along with Theodore Dick, on the Grand Mogul (Mine) deal to retire comfortably for life.

Col. Snowden died on August 10, 1907, at St. Louis, Missouri. He was 79 years old.

In June, 1907, Pete Orella moved his Standard Bottling Works into the old San Juan Livery barn behind Giacomelli's Iron Mountain Saloon.

Silverton dedicated its new Carnegie Library on July 25, 1906 (Fig. 127).

Fig. 127. **Now**-March, 1990 photo of the Carnegie Library-dedicated June 25, 1906. (Allan G. Bird photo)

Jonathon Fuller died on February 10, 1908. Fuller was a partner in the hardware firm of Crooke-Fuller & Company, which moved into the Posey & Wingate brick building in June, 1904, After Fuller's death, the firm was renamed Wm. H. Crooke & Company (Fig. 128).

A new city hall was begun in 1908. The original city hall on Blair Street, was completed in late 1883. After years of discussion, the new city hall was begun on the corner lots of the block that burned in 1890.

In July, 1908, William Brower was killed while hauling the red sandstone dimension rock for the city hall from the quarry, located on Mineral Creek. His team ran away while he was hauling a load of stone, weighing about five tons. The wagon rolled over and the rock landed on top of Brower. Construction was well under way by May, 1909,when one of the workers noticed that a small crack

Fig. 128. **Then**-Wm. H. Crooke Hardware Company in the Posey & Wingate building. c.a. 1910. (San Juan County Historical Society photo)

Fig. 129. **Now**-Site of the Crooke Hardware Co. (Allan G. Bird-August, 1998 photo)

had developed in the bell tower. The crack was rapidly growing wider. The street was roped off for safety. About 1:30 p.m., the entire tower, along with the upper story front wall, collapsed into the street. Construction was halted while experts were called to inspect the other walls. After a long delay, it was decided that the surviving walls would hold. Just as work was to resume, a thunderstorm in late

September washed out the railroad tracks, preventing the delivery of supplies. The building was not completed until August, 1910. On November 30, 1992, the building was gutted by fire. Ice-melting devices along the roof shorted out and the building burned from the top down. Because of the nature of the fire, all records in the safe were saved. The 1929 fire engine stored in the building was also saved, along with the jail. Several million dollars' worth of insurance and grants allowed the community to restore the structure to match its original appearance. Local craftsmen and labor did all of the work. After completion of the interior restoration, it was observed that the walls were bulging. Efforts were made to quarry new stone from the original quarry, however, this was not successful. Each stone was taken down and marked. If the stone had been damaged beyond saving, a mold was made and a mixture of cement and coloring was poured to match the color and texture of the original stone. Many of the stones now visible are artificial. State awards were received for the restoration effort.

Fig. 130. **Then**- March, 1990 photo showing the 1909 (Actually completed in 1910) Silverton Town Hall before the disastrous November 30, 1992 fire. (Allan G. Bird photo)

Fig. 131. **Now**-January, 1999 photo of the restored Silverton Town Hall. The roof and tower were destroyed and the interior gutted. (Allan G. Bird photo

The August 5, 1910 Labor Day parade (Fig. 123) contained some famous old-timers and history. Someone had written on the photo, "Mrs. Cotton-first woman. Frank Harwood, first boy born in Silverton." Frank Harwood died in 1906 before the Silverton Town Hall was built (visible in background). The September 10, 1910 *Silverton Standard* wrote the following description of the parade:

> The stagecoach was the original coach used between Del Norte and Silverton, before the advent of the railroad. Charlie Rew, the owner of the coach, is holding the gun that he used to ward off Indians and robbers in the old days. Mrs. Cotton was one of the occupants. The entry won first prize in the parade.

A contract was let to Arthur Castonguay on August 13, 1908, for the construction of the new Miner's Union Hospital (Fig. 132) on the site of Col. Snowden's 1874 cabin. In past years, Silverton had several small hospitals, usually run by individual doctors. With the heavy increase in mining, a large modern hospital was a necessity. Mine accidents were a weekly occurrence before the days of mine-safety training and enforcement. The new hospital was opened on June 7, 1909. The first four patients were: two miners who were thrown from Silver Lake aerial tramway bucket into ice-filled Silver Lake, a miner suffering from pneumonia, and a Globe, Arizona miner suffering from rheumatism.

Fig. 132. **Now**-1998 photo of 1907 Miner's Union Hospital. (Allan Bird photo)

On August 17, 1908, Jack Slattery, owner of the Hub Saloon, bet Neil McQueig $250 that he could not run to the top of Kendall Mountain, 4,000 feet above town, and return in one hour and 30 minutes. McQueig accepted the challenge and failed by one minute and 42 seconds. On Labor Day, Myron McWright, a young man scarcely 21, challenged McQueig's record and won, making the round trip in 1 hour, twenty-seven minutes, and twenty-five seconds.

About three weeks later, McWright entered the Hub and began drinking heavily. He bet some of the men in the bar $60 that he could make the trip in one hour and thirty minutes, starting at 6 o'clock in the evening. The weather was turning worse. It began to rain and snow on the mountain. The men tried to talk him out of the challenge, but he insisted. When he didn't return by 8 o'clock, search parties were formed to look for him. His frozen body was found early the next morning, hanging upside-down along the face of a cliff above timberline. His foot was wedged in a rock crevice.

The two old pioneer buildings, north of the Bausman building, were torn down in mid-April, 1909. Wm. Rogers owned Ed Lussy's shoe store. Wm. Cole owned C. H. H. Kramer's old meat market building, originally Tom Blair's Assembly Rooms. Cole left his lot vacant. Rogers built a substantial stone building for rental purposes. The owners of the Uno Club (located in the Robin building on the corner south of the hotel) opened the L & C Bar on August 2, 1909 in Rogers' new building. After a new stone foundation was installed, the vacated room in the old Robin building was taken over by Dr. Blair for use as a drug store. He was B. A. Taft's successor. Rogers' new building was divided into two sections, one a saloon, the other, a jewelry store. A disastrous fire almost destroyed the building during the early morning hours of July 2, 1911. At that time, it was occupied by George Noll's Palace Saloon and L. 0. Bastian's Confectionery Store. By the middle of August, the building was repaired and rented to the Landry Brothers Frog Saloon, formerly located in the Teller House building. When Prohibition hit Colorado on January 1, 1916, the Rogers building, occupied by the Frog Saloon, soon became empty. Wm. Miller, previous owner of the Gem Theater, on April 1, 1916, opened the new Star Theater after renovation from a saloon to a movie house. The Gem Theater, which was located just north of 11th on the west side of Greene Street, was a stiff competitor. The Gem offered $500 cash prizes over a six month period. Two weeks after the cash offer was made, the Gem was torched by some unknown parties and heavily damaged by fire. Mr. Maguire, the town of Silverton, and San Juan County offered a $500 reward for information leading to the arrest of the arsonist. No one was ever convicted. (Do you suppose the owner of the Star knew something about it?)

John Lorenzon, owner of the old Chicago Saloon, purchased one-half interest in the Star for his son, Arthur, on July 1, 1916. Lew Haas was their partner. Haas sold out to Lorenzon in late December, 1917. He moved to Denver to join his cousin in the automobile business. Haas was killed in an auto accident in mid-October, 1921.

J. V. Lorenzon owned a panoramic camera, which would take sweeping photos that were six inches wide and three feet long. Many prints are still in existence. In 1986, the camera was in the possession of his son, Eddie, who died a short time later. This camera was reported to be one-of four working models left in the world.

The Gem Theater was quickly rebuilt. To counter the Gem's cash prize lure, Lorenzon offered prizes of hand-painted panoramic photos of Silverton. The Star was extensively remodeled in late October, 1916, having the floor lowered and a confectionery and cigar stand installed in the lobby. On May 22-23, 1917, the Star featured the movie "Civilization" (Fig. 133). This supposedly was one of the greatest moves ever made. The *Silverton Standard* wrote the following review:

Thomas Ince produces his soothing, yet virile, argument against the common practice of war. Havoc wrought by an unseen submarine on a great ocean liner crowded with innocent souls, who are sent to the bottom without warning.

Then as a fitting climax to the harrowing scene, he makes a hero of the commander of the subsea craft by compelling him to sink his nefarious craft rather than repeat the despicable deed. All this, mind you, is actually shown on the screen. You first see the giant liner struck, then flounder, and finally sink. Then another ship approaches, all is made ready and, just as the fateful torpedo is to be fired, the commander is inspired to reform and when opposed by his comrades, opens the flood gates and all go down together. It is thrilling beyond description.

They didn't hide the punch line in those days. The normal 15-cent adult ticket was raised to 50 cents, with reserved seats going for 75 cents. The Star later became the Gem Theater. The original Gem Theater was built in 1910 and was located two doors south of the present Brown Bear Restaurant. The last movie house to occupy the building was the Lode. The last picture show was in February, 1990. Today, (1999) Michael Darr's Silver San Juan Art Gallery occupies the building.

Fig. 133. **Then**-Star Theater presentation of *Civilization*. Shown May 22-23, 1917. On the west side of Greene Street, north of 13th Street. (Eddie Lorenzon photo)

Fig. 134. **Then**-1990 photo of the old Star Theater, now the Lode. Movie house closed in 1984. Last movie was in February, 1990, when the historical society gave a benefit showing of *Ticket To Tomahawk*, the first major film made in Silverton, produced in 1949. Building renovated to become an art gallery today. Note the W. C. Rogers sign at the top of the building is gone. (Allan G. Bird photo)

Fig. 135. **Now**-August, 1998. Old Star Theater building. Now the Silver San Juan Art Gallery. Note that the W. C. Roger's sign has been replaced. (Allan G. Bird photo)

The name of the Grand Hotel was changed to the Imperial Hotel on July 3, 1909. The name was again changed during the early 1950's to the Grand Imperial Hotel.

August 27, 1910 marked the beginning of the end for frontier Silverton. The first automobile arrived over Stony Pass (Fig. 136). County Commissioner Louis Wyman, Dr. D. L. Mechling, and J. A. McGuire, editor of the Outdoor Life Magazine of Denver, drove from Lake City to Silverton. Dr. Mechling, former druggist for Fleming's Drug Store, owned the Croxton-Keeton 4 cylinder, 30-hp. vehicle. Dr. Mechling bought the car in Massalon, Ohio and drove it to Denver over prairie trails. He picked up Mr. McGuire in Denver, along with his young son. Wyman and Mechling were the best of friends and Mechling's son spent his summers living with Louis Wyman's family. Wyman had a son, Louis Jr., who was the same age as Eugene (Tug) Mechling. After days of struggling and help from Wyman, a semi-passable road was constructed near the top of Stony Pass for the car to travel on. They had to be pulled by horses over one particularly difficult stretch.

Their arrival in Silverton was marked by the explosion of dynamite and the ringing of the city hall bell, followed by a reception in front of city hall. John V. Lorenzon, photographer and part owner of the Chicago Saloon, built the road for auto traffic. The vehicle continued on to Yellowstone Park from Silverton.

Fig. 136. **Then**-Silverton's first automobile. This Croxton-Keeton 4 cylinder, 30 hp. roadster arrived in Silverton on August 27, 1910. Owned by Dr. Mechling in driver's seat. Louis Wyman is in the passenger seat. Eugene (Tug) Mechling, his son, is in the back seat. Dr. Mechling was an early citizen of Silverton. He worked with Mr. Fleming in the drug store. (San Juan Co. Hist. Soc. photo)

In mid-March, the Silverton Supply Company sold out to the Graden Mercantile Company of Durango. Graden moved into the old Perrung building, occupied by the Silverton Supply Company. They remained there for a short time, later moving into the Wyman building. Any photos showing the Silverton Supply Company were taken prior to March, 1917.

During the latter part of April, 1917, Robert Pearson moved the Consolidated Silverton Meat & Produce Company (Fig. 77) (now the Brown Bear Restaurant) into the building on the northwest corner of 11th and Greene, formerly occupied by Bert Brown's meat market (now a vacant lot). Robert Pearson was killed in an automobile accident near Salida in early July, 1921.

John Curry, the pioneer founder of the *La Plata Miner*, died during the week ending April 29, 1911. He died in the Old Soldiers' Home at Monte Vista. He had been blind for the past two years. He was 65 years old at the time of his death.

The old school house (Fig. 137), built in the fall of 1884 with a $10,000 bond issue, was torn down in late May, 1911. Work began immediately on the new brick school building (Fig. 139) in use today.

Fig. 137. **Then**-The old schoolhouse, completed in the fall of 1884. Torn down in late May, 1911. Building was facing Snowden Street. It was located on the present school playground, (Eddie Lorenzon photo)

During 1912, most of the wooden sidewalks along Greene Street were replaced with concrete. These sidewalks, according to Earnest Hoffman Jr., were partially paid for by the monthly fines levied against the gamblers and prostitutes of Blair Street.

Fig. 138. 1909 photo, showing the 1884 schoolhouse on the lower right-hand corner. The building was demolished in 1911. Looking east. (Colo. Hist. Society photo)

Fig. 139. **Now**-August, 1990 photo of the 1912 brick school. The old 1884 wooden school occupied the playground area adjoining the present school. (Allan G. Bird photo)

Fig. 127

On March 1, 1913, Dr. M. M. Blair sold his corner drug store (The 1890 Robin building) to the Rexall Drug Company, changing the name to the Rexall Pharmacy (Fig. 140).

Fig. 140. **Then**-West side of Greene Street south of 12th Street. Rexall Pharmacy occupied the corner building on March 1, 1913. c.a. early 1920's. (Eddie Lorenzon photo)

Fig. 141. **Now**-August, 1998 photo of the same scene as Fig. 140. Building on the far left was completed in 1998. Old Robin building is on the corner. Former home of the Uno Clubrooms around the turn of the century. The Uno had Silverton's first slot machines. (Allan G. Bird photo)

During the summer of 1913, John Melton, builder and owner of the "Big Brick Barn," later the Patterson Livery Stable, returned to his old building and opened the "Route Garage," Silverton's garage. Melton, along with his partner,

I. J. Bradford, had a Ford and a five-passenger Chalmers, which they rented during the summer months. The rate for three passengers was 40 cents per mile or $4 per day. Each additional passenger was one-third extra. Standing time was $1 per hour.

Construction on the new "Circle Route" state highway to Durango began during the summer of 1913. (Fig. 142) The road was not completed until early October, 1920.

Fig. 142. **Then**-Construction began on the Silverton-Durango "Circle Route" highway during the summer of 1913. The road was completed in October, 1920. The photo was taken about 1913. Silverton is in the open space at the far upper right. (Tom Savich photo)

Fig. 143. **Then**-Early 1920's photo of the new state highway. Note it is one-lane wide. Silverton is to the upper right. Silverton is in the upper right. (Tom Savich photo)

Fig. 144. **Now**-State Highway 550 in March, 1990. Photo taken in approximately the same area as Fig. 143. (Allan G. Bird photo)

A near-fatal shooting took place in late January, 1914. The trouble took place in Louis Giacomelli's Iron Mountain Saloon. Problems arose between two Slavonic-Austrians, by the name of Dogan and Louis Vukovich, a Montenegrin who was attending bar for Giacomelli. The trouble was caused by the attentions of a little Italian girl. Nick and Dan Dolan roughed up Vukovich. Both were arrested and jailed for threatening Vukovich's life and disturbing the peace. That night, William Dogan, a cousin of the two jail inmates, entered the saloon by way of the back door. Bent on revenge, he shot Vukovich at close range in the right jaw. The bullet shattered the bone knocked out a number of teeth, lodging in his neck near the jugular vein. Dogan tried to shoot him a second time, but was grabbed from behind by one of the bystanders. His .38-caliber revolver was wrenched from his hand. During the melee, someone unknown fired three other shots. Two of the shots hit Dogan, one in the back of the neck, entering below the right ear and coming out three inches to the left. The second shot hit him in the small of the back. The third shot hit a bystander in the right hand, between the thumb and first finger, lodging about six inches from the ceiling. All of the men lived. Dogan was sentenced to four-to-eight years at Canon City.

In March, 1914, snow caved in the roof of the Fulton Market (Fig. 145), formerly occupied by Blumfield's Photo Studio. The building was torn down and never replaced. On July 29, 1916, the Blumfield Studio next door, burned to the ground. These lots are directly south of the Wyman Hotel and both remain vacant. The original Fulton Market was one door south of the wooden frame building that caved in. It occupied a brick building (Fig. 145), which was in use until the mid-1990's when snow caved in the roof and brick front of the building.

Fig. 145. **Then**-1909 photo showing the location of the businesses on the west side of Greene Street, south of 14th Street. By 1914, Fulton moved next door into Blumfield's Studio and Blumfield moved into the Crystal Palace Saloon building. Both the latter buildings were destroyed and never replaced. The original Fulton Market, shown in photo, lost its roof and brick front to heavy snow in the mid-1990's. (Earnest Hoffman photo)

Fig. 146. **Now**-August, 1998 photo of the west side of Greene Street, south of 14th Street. The two vacant lots to the south of the Wyman building were the former sites of Fulton's Market and Blumfield's Photo Studio. For years, Blumfield's was occupied by the Crystal Palace Saloon. (Allan G. Bird photo)

January 1, 1916 brought Prohibition to Silverton. The County Club Saloon in the Benson building was closed. The Vienna Cafe, which had been a landmark in Silverton since shortly after the Benson building was built, expanded into part of the space previously occupied by the County Club Saloon. The Senate Saloon became the Rosemont Restaurant. The Hub Saloon switched to pool, billiards, and soft drinks, as did many of the other saloons. Silverton became a Mecca for bootleggers. For a short time, the local law enforcement officials cracked down on the illegal booze, but soon they were either bought off or gave up. After national Prohibition went into effect on January 16, 1920, the federal agents would make frequent raids on Silverton. Fortunately for the Silverton bootleggers, the road to Durango wasn't completed until October, 1920 and was closed by snow during the winter months. The only access to Silverton was by train. As soon as the agents would leave Durango, someone would phone Silverton and all of the bootleg joints were alcohol-free billiard parlors by the time the train arrived.

Town marshal, Charlie Leonard, maintained the Silverton law. He would round up all the able-bodied men to help move all the booze into the Rainbow Route Garage, now the T & T Market on Greene Street. Leonard also owned several of the cribs rented to prostitutes on Blair Street. On several occasions, the phone system failed. The February 18, 1928 *Silverton Standard* reported one such incident:

Find and Destroy 2500 gallons
Of Whiskey Mash

W. E. Lukens and John Simpson, federal enforcement officers for this district, were visitors in Silverton this week, and in going about the duties to which they were entrusted they made discoveries of several places where stills and the manufacture of intoxicants was in evidence, and when they had finished up their labors Thursday evening, they had destroyed some 2500 gallons of mash and 103 gallons of finished whiskey product.

The places that were visited were what is known as the Maple Place on lower Mineral Street, the old Ben Gilbert Carpenter Shop, the Motto House on upper Blair Street, a house on 14th Street and one on 10th and Empire. In making the search of the first and third places Lukens and Simpson were aided by Marshal Leonard and Sheriff Doud.

The coming of these men was not unknown to the folks here and as a consequence much mash and other articles were hidden out by those who hold same. Mr. Lukens and Simpson say they are going to keep coming as long as they are on the job, so it will be wise for those who are in this particular line of endeavor to be watchful and careful. No disturbance was created and the coming of the men was just a matter-of-fact daily occurrence.

An interesting side note of the above raid was the destruction of Silverton's milk supply for several days. It seems the agents dumped the confiscated mash into the local dairy's pasture and the cows feasted on the product and became thoroughly schnockered. The alcohol content was so high that the milk had to be destroyed.

Another danger of being caught selling or making bootleg whiskey was the government's practice of confiscating the furniture and fixtures of the saloons that were caught. The Bellview Saloon, (now Zhivago's Restaurant) had a beautiful hand-carved bar. Shortly after a successful raid, the feds announced they would confiscate the bar and all other fixtures. Phil Sartore was the owner at the time. He knew they would be up the following day to clean him out. To preserve his beautiful bar, he hired a crew to work through the night unbolting the bar and fixtures. That night, the entire furnishings of his Bellview Saloon were moved to a safe hiding place. The next morning the feds arrived and, in the words of Sartore, "They were mad as hell."

Francis Belmont's Mikado Saloon and Bordello on Blair Street was raided several times and the furniture confiscated by the feds. It was the practice of the government to auction off the furniture and fixtures to the highest bidder. The town folks would all band together and bid one cent on the dollar, with no one raising the bid. Often the entire auction would bring only $7 or $8. The end result was that Francis Belmont would end up with her furniture and fixtures by repaying the $7 or $8 paid by the people of Silverton.

Often the federal agents' zealous behavior would get out of hand. In one case, a young widow, whose husband died in the flu epidemic of 1918 when her baby was less than two months old, was caught making and selling wine to support herself and her young son. She was arrested and sent to the federal prison for two years.

In early January, 1918, F. W. Koehler moved his billiard hall from the 1876 Joseph Lacombe building to the corner store of the Imperial Hotel (now occupied by an Indian curio shop). Nondo Giacomelli moved his shoe repair store into the building after Koehler left.

October, 1918 brought Silverton's darkest hour. School was suspended from October 1 through the 21st pending development of the Spanish Flu. The disease struck Silverton with a vengeance about October 15. The October 26, 1918 *Silverton Standard* reported:

> Worst week ever known in the history of San Juan County, 42 dead.

By November 2, 128 deaths were reported. Before the plague ended in mid-December, 152 people or 12 percent of the population had died. Silverton had the highest per-capita death rate of any town in the nation. The undertaker, Mr. McLeod and his sister both died on the same day. The late Mary Swanson, long-time owner of Swanson's Market on Blair Street, lost her mother and brother on the same day, leaving her an orphan with three small brothers to support. She was 16 years old. People were dying so fast that they had to be buried in a mass grave. The Silverton Town Hall was made into a hospital. Many were taken to the pest house (located where the reclaimed tailing ponds north of town now stand). The late

Julia Maffey told the author that she remembered, as a small girl, looking out the upper windows of the Teller House and seeing wagons stacked with bodies heading for the cemetery. The town quarantine was finally lifted on December 21, 1918.

In November 1919, the Golden Rule Store, a branch of J. C. Penney's original store, bought out B. Van Slyck's clothing store, located in the present dining room and bar of the Grand Imperial Hotel.

In mid-January, 1920, the old Hub Billiard Hall was closed. The Benson Cafe, located across the street, moved into the space now occupied by the hotel lobby, and opened the American Café. The owner of the café was a good friend of "21" Pearl, one of the prostitutes and madams on Blair Street. He screened off a special section of his café for the prostitutes, who were allowed on Greene Street only between the hours of 4 and 6 p.m. to pick up their mail and have dinner.

In late March, the Cunningham Drug Store next to the hotel, sold out to Rexall. Rexall continued to operate this store, along with the store in the Robin building across the street to the south of the hotel.

In May, 1920, Henry Gray and Lew Parcell opened a new auto garage. They purchased the large brick and stone building south of the "Big Brick Barn" and combined the two buildings. Lew Parcell died in March, 1990, at the age of 101. He also managed the Silverton Electric Light Company.

Amanda Weed Cotton, the last of the 1874 pioneers, died on October 27, 1920 from a broken hip suffered a few days before in Cortez, Colorado.

1921 was a depression year for Silverton. The Miner's Union Hospital was forced to close because of financial difficulties. It reopened at a later date. Sam Wittrow, who had occupied the Bausman building for 17 years, was forced out of business. Many of the mines were closed because of low metal prices.

Part of our journey through old Silverton ends on December 31, 1921. Many buildings have vanished since 1921 and new ones have been built, however, the general appearance of Greene Street is little changed from 1921. The Fashion Theater was torn down during the 1920's. This was the last building on that side of the street to go, with the exception of the removal of the second story of the Exchange Livery building in the 1930's.

Joe Bordealeau's large hardware store, which occupied the three lots north of the Helmboldt building (Brown Bear Restaurant building), was torn down in the early 1970's. Brent Westlund completed a new structure on the northern two lots in the spring of 1998. John Perrung's building collapsed from snow in the mid-1970's, now replaced by the Silverton Minerals and Gifts Shop building with the bay window on the second story. Smedlley's Ice Cream Parlor was built during the 1970's. The post office is now on the northeast corner of 12th and Reese Streets.

During the 1930's, Silverton experienced its first airplane landing (Fig. 147). Some daredevil pilot decided to visit downtown Silverton and put his plane down on the highway on the south end of town. All the streets in Silverton were gravel at the time and it stirred up much dust and interest. The whole town came out to see what was going on. Happily, he was able to take off without meeting one of the nearby mountains. During the 1960's and early 1970's, Silverton had an airstrip north of town, just beyond the campgrounds where the highway now passes the reclaimed tailing ponds.

Before we close this chapter, the author believes strongly that a picture is worth a thousand words. Several of the interesting photos of Silverton during the 1920's and later follow:

Fig. 147. **Then**-c.a. 1936 photo of plane taking off on south Greene Street. (Tom Savich photo)

Fig. 148. **Then**-Early 1930 ambulance on the way to the mine meeting an ore truck on the way to the mill. (Tom Savich photo)

Fig. 149. **Then**-Early 1950 photo, judging from style of car on road. An exciting ride for the bus passengers. (Tom Savich photo)

Fig. 150. **Then**-The bus being pulled back on the road. (Tom Savich photo)

Fig. 151. **Then**-Summer, 1929 photo of Greene Street looking south. Note the two-story Exchange Livery on the far left. A garage occupies the north rooms of the Benson building. Vacant lot where the Temple of Fashion Saloon once stood. (Jim Bell photo)

Fig. 152. **Then**-Photo taken probably around 1915, showing a rock drilling contest between miners. Corner of 12th and Greene Streets. (Eddie Lorenzon photo)

Fig. 153. **Then**-1934 or 1935 photo of firemen having a water fight on the 4th of July. (Eddie Lorenzon photo)

Silverton & Ouray Toll Road, Mt. Abram in Distance, Silverton, Colo.

Fig. 154. **Then**-Undated photo, probably in the 1890's, of the Million Dollar Highway between Silverton and Ouray. (Allan G. Bird collection)

The year, 1932, brought one of the worst snow blockades in Silverton history. The people of Silverton went without fresh food for 90 days. By the end of the blockade, most of the coal, upon which the town depended upon for heat, was gone. Coffee and flour supplies were exhausted. John Matties, son of the owner of the Welcome Saloon and Boarding House on Blair Street (now a gift shop adjacent to Natalia's 1912 Restaurant), told how his father kept the entire cellar under the boarding house full of coal. He had enough to keep most of his neighbors warm until the end of the blockade. Following are a series of photographs of those hard times:

Fig. 155. **Then**-Train bucking snow slide during 1932 blockade. (Jim Bell photo)

Fig. 156. **Then**-Five engines trying to buck through the deep snow-1932 blockade. (Jim Bell photo)

Fig. 157. **Then**-Benching the slide with shovels so the train will have room to buck the remaining snow. (Jim Bell photo)

Fig. 158. **Then**-If you can't push it, melt it. 1932 snow blockade in Animas River Canyon. (Jim Bell photo)

Fig. 159. **Then**-Needleton Slide, 12 miles below Silverton. Trains from Silverton got as close as possible to pick up the passengers. (Jim Bell photo)

Fig. 160. **Then**-Getting your luggage to Silverton the hard way. 1932 snow blockade. (Jim Bell photo)

Fig. 161. **Then**-April, 1932. First mail in 90 days from Ouray, unloading in front of post office. Old Star Theater at far left is now the Gem Theater. (Jim Bell Photo)

Fig. 162. **Then**-End of the 90 day snow blockade, April, 1932. Circle Route Garage is at the far right. The Benson building is in the foreground. The old Exchange Livery building still has two stories (to the left of the Benson building). (Jim Bell photo)

+ CHAPTER 4 +

SILVERTON-THEN AND NOW
NOTORIOUS BLAIR STREET
A Walking Tour

The author wrote a detailed book on Blair Street in 1987, revised in 1993, entitled *Bordellos of Blair Street*. In the original version of *Silverton-Then and Now*, published in 1990, Blair Street was omitted. The author felt that to make the new, revised edition complete, a summary examination of the various bordellos, then and now, should be included. This will be designed as a walking tour of Silverton's Red Light District.

In the early 1970's, one of the old-time miners, who worked for the author, when he was general manager of the Sunnyside Mine, recalled Blair Street when it was in its prime, during the early 1920's. The man was only a young boy at the time but he described it as: "A little Las Vegas, gambling, drinking, women, 24-hours a day, 7 days a week."

Most of the bordellos and cribs are now gone but many remain, disguised as gift shops and restaurants. Life for a woman during the early days of Silverton was hard at best. Their choices of occupations were limited to sewing, cooking in the boarding houses, teaching school, or preferably, wives. There were no welfare checks to fall back on if hard times hit. If their husbands were killed in the mines or elsewhere, many were forced to enter a life of prostitution or face starvation.

The ratio of men to women in early Silverton was about 18 to 1. Most of the men were single or had left their wives in the old country while they tried to carve a new life in America. Many of the early miners were from Cornwall, England, a strong tin-mining area. The earliest came from Germany, Sweden, Finland and Wales. About the turn of the century, an influx of cheap labor came from near the Austrian-Italian border provinces of Tyrol, Austria and Piemonte, Italy. Others came from the Slavic countries. The Austrian-Italians and their families took over most of the bordellos, boarding houses and saloons on Blair Street by 1900. For years, there were strong feuds between the Austrians and Italians. Italians ran most of the businesses north of 12th Street. The Austrians controlled the area south of 12th Street. Many of Silverton's citizens today are descendants of these early settlers.

As was reported in earlier sections of this book, most of early prostitution was centered in the saloons and dance halls of Greene Street. Jane Bowen and her husband, William, ran the Westminster Hall, on the corner where the large, brick Benson building now stands. Tom and Pat Cain ran the Odeon Dance Hall, a few doors to the south. "Broncho" Lou ran the short-lived Diamond Saloon near the corner of 11th and Greene Streets.

Ordinances were passed as early as 1879 forbidding gambling and prostitution. Fines were assessed for both vices. The early ordinances were a form of legal extortion. The city fathers had no intention of banning the vices they made ordinances against. This allowed them to impose monthly fines against the gamblers and prostitutes, thus eliminating the need for property taxes to run the town. The usual fine was $35 a month for gamblers and $5 for prostitutes.

On July 28, 1884, a new ordinance was passed forbidding dance halls west of the alley between Greene and Blair Streets. The fine for violation of this ordinance was $300. From this day on, Blair Street became Silverton's sin street.

A few small establishments operated on Blair Street long before the 1884 ordinance. Alice Morris operated the oldest surviving bordello in Silverton (Fig. 163). The building was built in 1877. On September 16, 1878, county records show that Ernest Stephen, Jr. sold lot 15 to Alice Morris for $175. She sold the place to Alice Hanke on October 8, 1880 for $300. Alice ran it as a one-woman crib until 1882. Alice sold the building to Jacob Schneider, who used it as a residence for many years. He also purchased a crib two doors to the north and made it into a carpenter shop. The present Professor Shutterbug's Old Tyme Photo Studio (Fig. 164), across the street from the Bent Elbow Restaurant, contains the original building. A false front has been added in recent years and the back portion of the building was brought in from the ghost town of Middleton about 1950.

Fig. 163. **Then**-1883 photo showing Alice Morris's early crib, (arrow) later occupied by Alice Hanke. The Sherwood rental building is the large building at the left. Little is known about this building. The Diamond Saloon is directly behind Alice Morris's "house." (Colorado Historical Society photo)

Fig. 164. Now-Oldest surviving bordello on Blair Street. Alice Morris's 1878 "house." (Allan G. Bird photo-August, 1998)

As we walk north on the west side of Blair Street from 11th Street, the next building of historic interest is the original home of Lola Daggett. Lola was black and was known by the politically incorrect name of "Nigger" Lola. She purchased the small house on the north edge of Old Town Square. The buildings within the square are all of fairly recent origin. E. L. Roberts built the house in 1896. It was occupied by a series of prostitutes until Lola purchased it on November 20, 1920. Lola was born in northern Colorado and was raised in Pueblo. She arrived in Silverton about 1904. She had several black girls working for her out of this house. During the late 1920's, Lola moved about three doors up the street to a slightly larger house next to the present day Natalia's 1912 Restaurant. She added more girls to her staff and kept a black lady-pianist working full time.

Lola had a sister named Freda. Freda was a mulatto. When John Matties was a small boy, about 3 or 4, he remembered hearing his father talk about Freda, saying she was half-white. He was caught peeking into her doorway trying to see which half of her was white. Freda died in 1912 at the age of 35.

It is reported that one of her customers asked if the black ever rubbed off? She answered that, "If it did, there wouldn't be a business man in Silverton that would dare go home."

Lola became friendly with Rosa Stewart, the owner of the Avon Hotel. Many of the girls of Blair Street would frequent the coffee shop in the Avon as they were allowed on Greene Street only during restricted hours. Lola took sick in 1939 and Rosa cared for her. When she died on November 26, 1939, Lola willed all of her earthly belongings to Rosa Stewart. She is buried in Hillside Cemetery

Fig. 165. **Then**-1914 photo showing Lola Daggett's two bordellos on Blair Street. The second house has been demolished. (Eddie Lorenzon photo)

Fig. 166. **Now**-August, 1998 photo of Lola Daggett's first house on Blair Street. The log slabs were added much later. Building was built in 1896. (Allan G. Bird photo)

Page 146

north of town.

Two doors to the north from Lola's place was the Bon Ton, one of Blair Street's larger bordellos (Fig. 167). Robert Roberts constructed the building in 1884. Roberts rented the building to a madame by the name of Mable Pierce. Mable acquired enough money to purchase the building and land in 1889. In 1892, she borrowed $1,400 from Henry Sherman, a local blacksmith. The 1894 tax rolls show the land being owned by Mable Sherman. That's one way to eliminate a debt. By 1899, Roberts again owned the building. He sold it to Dottie Watson for $3,200. Two years later she was judged insane and sent to Pueblo to the state mental hospital. Word was received shortly after her arrival that she had only weeks to live. She was suffering from syphilis of the brain.

Shortly after Dottie acquired the building, she borrowed $2,100 from Mary Kloster, a local realtor. Needless to say, she defaulted on her note. Mary leased the property to numerous women. In the 1930's, it was a restaurant and rooming house. The building burned to the ground in 1945.

Fig. 167. **Then**-1914 photo of the Bon Ton Bordello. (Eddie Lorenzon photo)

Fig. 168. **Now**-Site of the Bon Ton. (Allan G. Bird-Aug., 1998 photo)

Next door, to the north, of the Bon Ton, was "Nigger" Lola's second house. Adjacent to Lola's was one of the earlier large bordellos, the Nell Castell House (Fig. 169). John Curry, editor and owner of the *La Plata Miner* newspaper, built the building in 1883. In July, 1888, Curry sold it to one of the "soiled doves" by the name of Nell Castell. Nell was mentioned in the earlier chapters when she went after Frank Cooper, the bartender of the Hub Saloon, with a clasp knife. After a year, Nell defaulted on her mortgage and the house was vacant for several years. In 1894, Jack Matties purchased the building. Louisa Crawford purchased the lot where Lola's future second house was to be. Matties and Crawford were married in 1897 and Louisa ran the old Nell Castell house. It became know as Louisa's Dance Hall.

In March, 1897 a fight took place in the dance hall which required the services of a physician. The paper reported that three Italians cut each other up. Joe Sartore quickly replied in the press that "the men were Austrians, not Italians. Italians are peaceable and seldom fight." This was the first reference to the Austrian-Italian feud.

Jack built a lean-to on the north side of the old building and opened the Welcome Saloon. Jack and Louisa prospered and became quite wealthy. Louisa ran about 12 or 13 girls while Jack tended the bar. All went well until 1903.

Jack Matties was a rather boisterous man and liked to flaunt his wealth. He sold the dance hall to his brother, Battiste, in 1901 for $6,000; the highest price paid for any building on Blair Street up until that time. Jack decided to return to his homeland in Trento, Tyrol, Austria for a visit, taking about $5,000 in gold coin with him. In November, 1903 they found his body in a river adjacent to the railroad tracks in what is now Monaco. He was robbed, murdered, and his body thrown from the train. After his death, Louisa cleared out the girls from the bordello and lived there alone. Louisa became somewhat of a recluse, eventually retiring to Chicago. She deeded all of her interest in the Welcome Saloon to her brother-in-law.

In 1909, Battiste tore down the old Welcome Saloon lean-to and added the large addition, now occupied by Natalia's 1912 Restaurant. He opened his new Welcome Saloon (Fig. 170) with the finest bar on Blair Street.

At the age of 38, Battiste returned to Tyrol, Austria and married a 17-year-old waitress whom he met in a restaurant. She returned with him and ran a "boarding house" for years in the old bordello. Her two sons, Joe and John, both swore that mother ran only a boarding house, however, the late Annie Smith remarked, when seeing an old photo of the building that, "that was the biggest hookshop on Blair Street. Mrs. Matties told me she had 35 girls working at one time."

This was one of the problems of doing research on the Red Light District of Silverton, no one wanted to admit that grandma ran a whorehouse.

During the deadly flu epidemic of 1918, the building became a hospital. Battiste made a broth of chicken soup and red wine and fed it to all of his patients. He lost only one girl, Bessie Miller, the sister of "Sheeny" Pearl, both prostitutes. Both his wife and two sons became deathly ill from the flu, but all survived.

Battiste died in April, 1924. The property remained in the family until 1947, when his sons sold it for $5,000. For years it served as a garage and storage facility.

Fig. 169. **Then**-1883 photo showing the new 1883 Nell Castell House. The small building on the far right was built in 1883 by Theodore Dick as a rental one-girl crib. It was used as a crib until 1907. (Eddie Lorenzon photo)

Fig. 170. **Then**-Photo taken in 1949. Note the old roofline of the Nell Castell House where it joins the 1909 Welcome Saloon addition. (Jim Bell photo)

Fig. 171. **Then**-1909 photo of Battiste Matties in his new Welcome Saloon bar. Note the antique slot machine on the right side of the bar. (Ed Boracio photo)

Fig. 172. **Now**-August, 1998 photo of the old Nell Castell House **on the** left and the 1909 Welcome Saloon on the right. The original 1883 Nell Castell House has been covered with stucco. (Allan G. Bird photo)

Jane Bowen, or the "Sage Hen" as she was affectionately called, built a residence for her and her husband directly behind their Westminster Hall Dance Hall in 1880. It was originally 25 by 60 feet in size. After the 1884 ordinance moving all dance halls to Blair Street, they increased the size to the full length of the lot, 100 feet. This then became the dance hall and bordello. The architecture was less than dramatic. The building resembled a World War II Army barrack.

In 1892, after William Bowen's death, Jane sold her establishment to Joseph Sartore. In 1894, Sartore sold half-interest to Ludwig Vota for $750. Vota took over management of the business. The newspapers referred to it as Ludwig's "pest house."

In 1900, Sartore and Vota leased the building to "Billy" Luke. Luke's establishment had the reputation of a place that "could be dangerous to your health." Luke operated as a gambling hall and bordello for 25 years. The papers reported several suicides by the "soiled doves" working in Billy Luke's place. The favorite method of ending their miseries was by laudanum (heroin) or carbolic acid. A rather painful way to go.

On February 20, 1926, Angelina Sartore and Mary Vota, heirs of Joe Sartore and Ludwig Vota, sold the dance hall to a group of men that included John (Jack) Gilheany, Tom Gilheany, Charlie Longstrom, Tom Olson, and Sam Manuch, for $2,000. The place became known as the "Laundry." The late Jim Hook once said: "If you went in with any money, you came out clean." In 1928, Jack Gilheany bought out Longstrom and the others and operated until the early 1940's, when he moved to Greene Street.

Jack Gilheany was known to take half of a miner's loss and give it to their families for food. Some of these men would come from the mine and lose their entire paychecks before providing for their families. One lady interviewed stated that she never received any money from Gilheany after her husband lost his paycheck.

The back end of the building was removed in 1952 and the remainder in 1957 or 1958.

Fig. 173. **Then**-1914 photo showing Jane Bowen's 1880 residence and bordello. (Colo. Hist. Soc. photo)

Fig. 174. **Then**-1950 photo of the "Laundry." Jane Bowen's 1880 bordello. Sign "Blooms" was painted for a 1949 movie set. (Jim Bell photo)

Fig.175.**Then**-1927-Charlie Longstrom, in the white hat, dealing at the Laundry. (Carl Longstrom photo)

Fig. 176. **Now**-August, 1998 photo of High Noon Hamburger Stand that occupies the site of Jane Bowen's 1880 bordello. (Allan G. Bird photo)

Next door, to the north of the Laundry, was a small crib originally owned by Alice Morris. She moved into this building (Fig. 173) after she sold her original crib to Alice Hanke. In later years, Ludwig Vota increased the size of the building and it became part of his large bordello next door. In the 1930's, it was known as the Tree Top, a four-girl crib. The building was torn down in the late 1950's. It is now a vacant lot.

Next door to the Tree Top, was the Mikado. C. M. Frazier, one of Silverton's lawyers of questionable character, built a small crib on the lot in 1893. By 1925, a lean-to was added to the north side of the building. "21" Pearl Thompson purchased the building in 1925. She ran a bar in the south half and a bordello in the new lean-to. When the Mikado name was attached is not known, however, it was probably given by "21" Pearl. Pearl had a partner by the name of Francis Belmont. Together they ran the place. On February 13, 1928, Pearl committed suicide. The cause was never definitely determined, but it is believed that she overdosed on sleeping pills. Shortly before her death, she sold the building to W. H. Mowat for $1000. Mowat, in turn, sold it to Francis Belmont in 1934 with the provision that she pay the back taxes due for the years 1931, 1932, and 1933. Francis had leased the building during this time.

Francis Belmont was well liked by the people of Silverton. During the Depression, she left many bags of groceries on hungry doorsteps without ever telling the recipients where they came from. Francis died of cancer in 1936.

After Francis Belmont's death, "Big Billie" (Betty Wagner) took over the operation of the Mikado. She had several girls working for her, including Ollie Kelly and "Babe" or "Blonde Peggy." Babe eventually married one of the local boys.

Nick Bonaventura bought the building at a tax sale and used it to store bakery equipment. The structure was destroyed by fire in 1954.

Fig. 177. **Then**-1949 photo of the Mikado Saloon and Bordello. The building burned in 1954. The left portion was built in 1893, the right portion in 1925. The right half was the bordello. (Jim Bell photo)

Fig. 178. **Now**-August, 1998 photo of the Lookout building, site of the former Mikado Saloon and Bordello. (Allan G. Bird photo)

The two lots north of the Mikado, now a gift shop and park, were used by the Exchange Livery as a corral for their horses.

The 1883, Silverton City Hall building is next. This building has been discussed in earlier chapters.

Next to the city hall, is the Stone Saloon, built in 1897 by Joe Todeschi. In 1901, the property was sold to Jack Matties at a sheriff's sale. Matties sold the building back to the Todeschi Brothers and Domenica Dallavalle for $1,528.33. In 1902, there was a shooting in the building, in which Peter Dalla was shot in the leg and seriously injured. The complete story of Peter Dalla is written in the author's book, *Bordellos of Blair Street*.

The building was also used as a crib by several women, including "Black Minnie" Heberline. She was white but her disposition was black. Rose Lane also worked out of this building. She later bought a crib near the present Bent Elbow Restaurant.

Today the building serves as a gift shop.

Fig. 179. **Now**-August, 1998 photo of the 1897 Stone Saloon and Bordello. (Allan G. Bird photo)

Next door to the Stone Saloon to the north, is the present Dallavalle Bed and Breakfast Hotel. Domenica Dallavalle, later shortened to Dalla, built this building in 1902. The rock was laid by unemployed Tyrolian stone masons from rock quarried near the mouth of Cement Creek, north of town.

Shortly after completion of the building, John Dalla, Domenica's husband, opened the Tyrolian Saloon. He died of frostbite driving cattle over Molas Pass during the winter. They had eleven children at home. Domenica operated a boarding house on the east bank of Cement Creek.

After John Dalla's death, the property was leased to a man named Minolla, who operated the saloon. The building was used for a saloon until local Prohibition in 1916. After the saloon closed, the building was used as a boarding house.

Domenica Dalla died, along with two of her sons, during the 1918 flu epidemic. Mary, her 16-year-old-daughter, was left with three small brothers to raise. She continued to operate her mother's boarding house. Mary inherited the saloon property from her older brother.

In 1941, Mary, who was now married to a man named Swanson, borrowed $500 on an insurance policy to pay off back taxes on the saloon property. She had $25 or $35 left, which she used to open Swanson's Market. Her first purchase was a full beef, which she was able to buy on credit. She ground the entire beef and made Italian sausages, which she and her brothers sold door-to-door. They raised enough money to eventually stock the store. Mary died in the mid-1980's and her son, Gerald, operated the market until September 24, 1988. He closed the market and opened Swanee's Gift Shop. About the mid-1990's, he and his wife, Nancy, turned the building into the Dallavalle Bed and Breakfast Hotel.

Fig. 180. **Then**-1986 photo of Swanson's Market, the old Tyrolian Saloon, later the Minolla Saloon. Swanee's Gift Shop and the Dallavalle Bed & Breakfast Hotel followed Swanson's Market. (Allan G. Bird photo)

Fig. 181. **Now**-August, 1998 photo of the old Tyrolian Saloon, later the Minolla Saloon., now the Dallavalle Bed and Breakfast Hotel. (Allan G. Bird photo)

Very early in Silverton's history, a small residence occupied the vacant corner next to the Dallavalle Hotel. Later, three small buildings occupied the space, two owned by Mary Scheidt as a residence, the third by a blacksmith shop. On July 21, 1910, Caterina Giono bought the land for $1,400. Her husband, John Giono, pronounced Guy-no, built a large two-story frame saloon and boarding house covering the two corner lots. A lean-to kitchen was built on the lot next to the present hotel. He named his establishment the Piemonte Saloon and Boarding House (Fig. 182). It was a favorite boarding house for miners.

John Giono died in 1932. He died in Durango during one of the frequent snow blockades. It was over a month before his body could be returned for burial.

After his death, Martin and Paco Cina ran the saloon. Paco died, leaving the business to Martin. Martin had several prostitutes working for him. When he was there by himself, the girls would get him so drunk that he would pass out. They would then carry him to bed and open up the bar for a big party, drinking Martin's booze. This cost him dearly, as they were giving away all of his profits.

It is not known how long the saloon operated or when it closed. A man from Cortez, Colorado bought the building for back taxes in 1944 and tore it down for

Fig. 182. **Then**-1917 photo of John Giono's Piemonte Saloon on the southwest corner of 13th and Blair Streets, now a vacant lot. John Giono is in the white shirt. Photo includes 3 members of Silverton's African-American population. (Jim Bell photo)

the lumber.

North of 13th Street, three doors from the corner, stood the North Pole Saloon (Fig. 183). This was the last saloon and whorehouse on the west side of Blair Street. On May 3, 1902, Matt Chiono started building the North Pole Saloon. Chiono was originally a partner in the Iron Mountain Saloon with Louis Giacomelli. The building was completed in June, 1902. The original building was 24 X 60 feet in size. Later, in 1904, an additional forty feet was added to the rear of the building, thus covering the entire 100 feet of the lot. During the time the Chionos' owned the building, it was used as a saloon and boarding house. In the 1930's, several women worked out of this building. Annie Smith said that it was never a "hookshop." Corky Scheer replied: "The hell it wasn't. I was there."

In the mid-1970's, the building was leaning precariously toward the north. Today it is being restored.

Fig. 183. **Then**-1951-North Pole Saloon. (Jim Bell photo)

Fig. 184. **Now**-January, 1999 photo of old North Pole Saloon. (Allan G. Bird photo)

We will now cross the street and head south on the east side of Blair Street. Tom Cain's Dance Hall stood where the 1883 wooden jail now stands. Next door was Riley Lambert's Dance Hall and Saloon. By 1890, Lambert's building had been demolished and removed. In 1899, Louis Sartore built the Bellview Saloon and Boarding House. This building is occupied by Zhivago's Restaurant today.

Sartore died on March 17, 1901 from pneumonia. He left a wife and a son, Philip, who later took over the Bellview Saloon. The saloon was leased to John Giono in 1905. Giono built the Piemonte Saloon across the street, on the corner, in 1910.

Philip Sartore had come of age by 1910 and operated the Bellview for many years. During Prohibition, Sartore ran a moonshine still in the basement. He made his own whiskey and Zinfandel wine. He was "busted" several times by the Feds. He kept iron bars across his sink so in case of a raid he could quickly break the bottles of booze and eliminate the evidence. He commented "they couldn't arrest you for smelling it."

Mrs. Sartore had her residence and boarding house upstairs above the saloon. She charged $1 a day for board. Sartore ran the saloon for 38 years. He sold the property to John Troglia in 1948. During the 1950's, Jess Carey operated a museum on the main floor. It was used for several movie sets in the early 1950's. The sign, Red Ashes Saloon, (Fig. 158) was painted for a movie set.

The Bellview was never a bordello. Since the 1970's, the building has housed Zhivago's Restaurant.

Next door to the south, was a small house in which Peter Dalla was killed in September, 1904. He had been shot in the leg three months before, just before his scheduled wedding. By September, he was well enough to take his vows, when someone placed a bundle of dynamite on the outside of his small house, adjacent to his bed. At 3:30 in the morning, the building and Peter Dalla were blown to smithereens. This was the apex of the Tyrolian-Piemonte feud. Dalla was a Tyrolian and the girl he was to marry was from Piemonte. The full story of this incident is in the author's book *Bordellos of Blair Street.*

Fig. 185. **Then**-1954 photo of the 1899 Bellview Saloon. Sign on building was painted for a movie set. (Ruth Gregory photo)

Fig. 186. **Now**-1899 Bellview Saloon in August, 1998. (Allan G. Bird photo)

Three doors south of the Bellview Saloon is a small crib (Fig. 187), built about 1900 by C. C. H. Kramer, a local butcher. Many of the "proper" citizens of Silverton built rental units for the prostitutes. The building operated as a house of prostitution until 1916, when Barney Tocco and his wife purchased it and opened a "convenience and shoe store." They sold basic groceries and supplies along with shoes to the women of the "line." Tocco was from Piemonte, Italy. Barney died in 1937. His wife continued to operate the store until her death in 1951. Her newspaper ads always had the caption, "In memory of Barney Tocco."

Fig. 187. **Then**-1954 photo of 1900 crib. Barney Tocco's Piemonte Grocery Store occupied the building from 1916 until 1951. Now the Candle Shop. Sign was for a movie set. (Ruth Gregory photo)

Fig. 188. **Now**-August, 1998 photo of the 1900 crib. (Allan G. Bird photo)

Next door, to the south of Barney Tocco's old store, is a small crib built in 1897 (Fig. 189). For a short time after its construction, the Gold King Mining Company used the building as an office. In 1900, Gold King sold it to Louis Sartore. Sartore leased the building to prostitutes. Minnie Davis and Jose Alexander both worked out of this crib. In 1947, Louis Sartore's son sold the property to Jess Carey. Rosa Stewart, owner of the Avon Hotel, bought the land and building in 1950. Today it is a gift shop.

Fig. 189. **Then**-1954 photo of Louis Sartore's crib, built in 1897. It was rented to prostitutes for many years. The sign was used in a movie set. (Ruth Gregory photo)

Fig. 190. **Now**-August, 1998 photo of Sartore's crib. (Allan G. Bird photo)

The large, two-story brick building next to Sartore's crib was one of the larger bordellos and gambling halls on Blair Street. On January 8, 1907, Emma Roberts sold lots 7 and 8, along with 2 feet of lot 9 to John Mattivi for $1,700. The price would indicate that Roberts had already built the brick portion (Fig. 191) of the building before the sale. A large wooden bordello existed on lot 8, next to the brick structure. The Mattivi's bought both buildings in the deal. The frame structure was either destroyed by fire or torn down by 1912 or early 1913. Mattivi's named their business the Monte Carlo.

Corky Scheer remembered that "Jew" Rose worked there. In his words,"There were quite a number of girls in there. They were all young and tender. I've been thrown out of all of them." The Monte Carlo operated until about 1935. In 1949, the building was used as a bank in the movie, "Run for Cover," starring James Cagney. A false front was constructed on the building and then blown off with explosives during a staged bank robbery. In 1978, structural problems developed on the second floor of the building which necessitated removal of the original ornamental brick front of the building and replacing it with a plain brick front (Fig. 192). The lean-to on the south side of the building was a stable built by the Mattivis.

Fig. 191. **Then**-1954 photo showing the 1907 Monte Carlo Bordello and Gambling House. The sign "Bank" was for the 1949 movie, "Run for Cover," with James Cagney. (Ruth Gregory photo)

Fig. 192. **Now**-August, 1998 photo of old Monte Carlo Bordello and Gambling Hall. The old stable on the right has been converted into shops. (Allan G. Bird photo)

In the vacant lot to the south of the Monte Carlo, stood the Diamond Belle Dance Hall. This was a large, two-story frame structure built in 1902. A small crib occupied the space prior to 1902, owned by Louisa Crawford and Jack Matties, owners of the Welcome Saloon in the next block south. Matties and Crawford sold the lot and small crib to a French woman by the name of Louisa Maurell and her sister, Marie. The building had 12 rooms upstairs for the "dancers."

Louisa Maurell had rolled a blacksmith of $170 by plying him with drinks until he passed out. When he came to and found his money gone, he asked her to return it. She told him to get out, whereby he pulled a pocketknife and stabbed her twice, once in the back and once in the hip. He was arrested and sentenced to 20 days in jail. He never saw his money again.

This type of treatment didn't go well with the local miners and her business slacked off dramatically after the above incident. She was forced to sell the business to Fred McIlmoyle and J. A. Doucet. McIlmoyle tried to kill his wife shortly after he purchased the Belle and his partner took over the management. Both men defaulted on the mortgage they had taken from Louisa. By late 1903, she had the dancehall back.

She leased the hall to Tom Gross (Grosso) in 1906. He took off owing many debts around town. The management of the Belle again reverted to Louisa Maurell. She mortgaged the property to about 3 different insurance companies, using the Belle for collateral. In 1907 the Schirmer Insurance Company took over ownership of the building. They sold it to John Orella. John had recently operated the National the National Hall, which we will discuss shortly, for his brother Pete. Pete also owned the Standard Bottling Works. John operated the Belle until May, 1922. A series of owners kept the business operating as a bordello well into the 1930's.

Some of the more memorable names of the working girls were: Bertha "Kate" Starr, Billy Deboyd, Rose Rody and "Sheeny" Pearl Miller, the sister of Bessie Miller, one of the first 1918 flu fatalities.

The building was demolished in the 1940's.

Fig. 193. **Then**-1940 photo of the 1902 Diamond Belle Saloon and Dance Hall. **Now**-a vacant lot, two doors north of the Arcade Gift Shop. (Jim Bell photo)

On the corner, to the south, is the Arcade (Fig. 193). This is the most recent of the bordellos, built in 1929 during the Prohibition era. Officially it was the Arcade Recreation Hall. They served bootleg whiskey and kept several women in the back rooms. For years prior to 1929, the two corner lots contained 3 small wooden cribs. Francis Rawley built one of the oldest cribs in Silverton in 1882 on the lot north of the Arcade. C. A. Leonard, one of Silverton law enforcement officers, owned the two cribs on the corner lot. Leonard owned the cribs until 1920.

"Black Minnie" Heberline operated from one of these cribs. She later married Phil Sartore, owner of the Bellview Saloon. One of the cribs was "busted" for being an opium den.

Corky Scheer recalled, "They sold bootleg whiskey in the Arcade. "Big Billie" worked there. I once threw a rock at her and missed, breaking the window."

Fig. 194. **Then**-1954 photo of the 1929 Arcade Building. Cafe signs in the window were for a move set. (Ruth Gregory photo)

Fig. 195. **Now**-May, 1999 photo of the Arcade. Curved decoration on the top was recently added. It says 1920. This is in error, it was built in 1929. (Allan G. Bird photo)

The vacant lot, on the south, adjacent to where the train stops, once hosted one of the largest bordellos in Silverton. After Jane Bowen sold her 1880 Dance Hall, following her husband's death, she retired for two years. She returned and purchased the lot across the street on the southeast corner of 12th and Blair Street. There she built her new Palace Hall. The building was completed during the week ending August 13, 1892. Jane purchased the finest bar and fixtures for her new hall. She also bought a grand piano for $450 from a music store in Denver. All of her equipment and piano was purchased on the installment plan.

Jane gave a grand ball to celebrate her opening, in which the entire town was invited. The *Silverton Standard* commented that, "The lack of space prevents us from giving the names of all who attended." In other words, the "elite" of Silverton should not be attending the grand opening of a whorehouse.

In 1893, Jane purchased the adjoining lot to the south from Mrs. Murphy, owner of the Silverton Hotel. In 1895, she built a large addition to the original building on the new lot.

Jane continued to prosper in her new venture, however, all was not smooth. In 1893, John Louis, her nephew, who arrived from England only three weeks past, died in the dance hall. In 1895, while caring for another nephew from England, there was a minor misunderstanding and he became angry. He retaliated by putting carbolic acid in the food being served to Jane and her girls. She shipped him off to England on the next train.

Tragedy struck Jane in 1898, when her adopted daughter committed suicide in Denver by taking "Rough on Rats" poison. After her death, Jane decided to return to England for awhile. She leased the hall to Jack Matties from March 1, 1898 to March 1, 1900. It became known as Jack Matties's Dance Hall during this period.

After Jack's lease expired, the property was leased to Albert Swanson until Jane's return in February, 1902.

Jane "The Sage Hen" Bowen returned and operated the Palace until 1905, when she retired and sold the business to Peter Orella, owner of the Standard Bottling Works. Peter leased it to his brother, John Orella, and Vigilio Valdan. They changed the name of the business to the National Saloon and Hall.

A month before the lease was up, Peter Orella sold the business to Joe and Santina Corazza for $5,000. The Corazzas prospered in the National Hall. Mrs. Corazza made frequent trips to her homeland in Tyrol, Austria. She would buy diamonds while overseas and hide them in her knitting yarn. She became known as the local Silverton diamond merchant.

Joe Corazza died shortly before midnight on January 27, 1918. Mrs. Corazza continued to operate the hall until 1929 when she sold it to Mike Serra. During the 1930's and 1940's, the property passed through several hands.

From about 1935 until 1948, "Jew" Fanny Wright occupied the lower floor of the "new" 1895 addition. Fanny was the last prostitute to operate out of the National Hall. She was also the last prostitute to leave Silverton in 1948.

The building was used in several movie sets between 1949 and 1955. It was sold for taxes in the early 1950's. A heavy snowstorm crushed portions of the roof in 1952. Demolition crews finished the job in the late 1950's.

Fig. 196. **Then**-The National Hall. Photo was taken during a scene from the 1949 movie, "Ticket to Tomahawk." The balcony was added for the film. "Jew" Fanny occupied the rooms below the Hotel Esmeralda sign. (Don Stott photo)

Fig. 197. **Then**-1954 photo of Jane Bowen's 1892 Palace Hall, later the National Hall. The building was demolished about four years after this photo was taken. **Now**-a vacant lot next to the train stop. (Ruth Gregory photo)

Next door to the National Hall is a vacant lot that once hosted "Fatty" Collins' large wooden bordello and gambling hall. It was built in 1883. Collins died sometime between 1884 and 1887. The building was purchased by Emma Harris, the Russian princess, in 1890 and moved to Greene Street.

The next lot contained the Alhambra Theater, a combination saloon, gambling hall and variety theater. This was Silverton's first theater, built in 1883. The building burned to the ground on May 27, 1891. Two men were in the building at the time of the fire. Both jumped to safety: However, one had left his wallet with $60 in crisp new bills under the mattress. After the fire, while sifting through the ashes, the charred wallet was found with the money undamaged.

On June 12, 1897, Fred Barry built a four unit crib which, for a better name, I call the Green House (Fig. 198), as it has always been painted green. The is the front portion of the present Shady Lady Restaurant. Each unit was sold to a girl for $100, much like a condominium today. Minnie Haugh was the first tenant. By 1901, prices had dropped and Minnie Sanborn bought a unit for $35. In 1905, Ludwig Vota obtained ownership of the entire building. He leased the four rooms to women of the line until his death. The building remained with his family until 1937.

"Jew" Fanny rented the two units on the south side of the building before she moved to the National Hall in 1935. Fanny had one or two girls working with her most of the time. Other renters were Pearl Silas, Kate Starr, Mayme Murphy and many others over the years.

Today the building has added a balcony and a large extension to the rear of the original unit. It was a mystery for many years why there was a door on the upstairs level when there was no apparent use for it. It was later revealed by one of the former inmates that they used it to shake out their carpets.

Fig. 198. **Then**-1954 photo of Blair Street showing the "Green House" on the far left. The three buildings in the center were destroyed by fire on January 16, 1968. (Denver Pub. Library Western Hist. Collection photo)

Fig. 199. **Now**-August, 1998 photo of the "Green House." The balcony was recently added. The original building ended at the end of the sloped roof. (Allan G. Bird photo)

Mayme Murphy, like most of the women of the line, moved several times during her sojourn on Blair Street. In 1900, Ludwig Vota built a small crib (Figs. 198 & 200) next door, to the south, of the "Green House." Dozens of prostitutes occupied this building over the years; however, only two are remembered, Mayme Murphy and "Jew" Fanny. Mary Swanson remembered Mayme Murphy as, "an ornery old lady on the line, who would curse at the kids." Mayme met her end by plugging in a heating pad with a short circuit. After Mayme's death, "Jew" Fanny worked in this crib for a short time, before moving into the "Green House." The building burned to the ground on January 16, 1968.

Fig. 200. **Then**-1954 photo of Ludwig Vota's 1900 crib. (Ruth Gregory photo)

Next door to Mayme Murphy's crib was a similar building, also built by Ludwig Vota in 1897. One of the last prostitutes to occupy this building was Rose Lane. Rose had previously worked out of the small Stone Saloon building on the next block to the north. Jim Hook, Sr. remembered Rose as "Big Freda." After Silverton closed down its red light district, Rose married a mine blacksmith by the name of Carl Blake. They bought a ranch in Oklahoma and retired.

Dr. Holt, a local Silverton doctor, had a drinking problem. On January 16, 1968, it is believed that he fell asleep smoking a cigarette. The resulting fire destroyed the old crib and the two adjacent buildings next door.

Fig. 201. **Then**-1954 photo of Ludwig Vota's 1897 crib. Sign on building was used for a movie set. Building burned on January 16, 1968. (Ruth Gregory photo)

Next door to Vota's crib was one of the larger bordellos on Blair Street, the Tremount Saloon. W. S. Hung, the Chinese laundry man known as "Spider," who was forced to leave Silverton in 1902, last owned the original small building on this lot. He was able to salvage $350 by selling his land and building to Jack Slattery, owner of the Hub Saloon in the Grand Hotel.

Slattery leased the building to girls of the line to be used as a crib. On January 31, 1907, Jack Slattery sold the land and building to Matilda Wenden Fattor, affectionately known as "Big Tilly." Matilda was a large-framed woman weighing between 300 and 400 pounds. She was married to Celeste Fattor, a man less than half her size. "Big Tilly" built the two-story Tremount in 1907. She served as the Madame and bouncer of the bordello. The building had fourteen beds upstairs and a bar and dance floor on the main level.

"Big Tilly" contacted pneumonia and died on January 25, 1918, the same day as her neighbor to the north, Joe Corazza, owner of the National Hall. "Tilly" was 42 years old at the time of her death. She was a native of Sweden.

Celeste returned to his home in Italy and brought back a new wife. They continued to operate the Tremount until August, 1925. The property went through a series of owners until the Great Depression struck in October, 1929. Mrs. Sam Eccher had loaned the last owner, Gio Bari, $2,000. He defaulted on the loan and Mrs. Eccher became the new owner of the Tremount in 1933. The building was used as a liquor store with a small bar in the back. During the late 1930's and 1940's, it was converted into a boarding house for miners. Mrs. Eccher retained the building until 1952.

Frank Bostock purchased the building and opened the first Bent Elbow Restaurant. He sold the business to Effie Andreatta, who continued to operate the restaurant until the 1968 fire.

She moved two doors to the south and renovated the old Florence Saloon, which is today's Bent Elbow Restaurant. Mike Andreatta sold the restaurant in the spring of 1999.

Fig. 202. **Then**-"Big Tilly" Fattor's 1907 Tremount Saloon and Bordello. Girls are looking out of upstairs windows. "Tilly" is on the left. Her husband Celeste is in the white apron. Building burned in January, 1968. (Jim Bell Collection)

Fig. 203. **Then**-1954 photo of the Tremount Saloon. Cafe sign was for a movie set. Rose Lane's crib was on the left and the Fattor residence, later the Green Lantern, on the right. (Ruth Gregory photo)

Next to the Tremount Saloon, was the early residence of "Big Tilly" and Celeste Fattor. During the 1920's, Fattor's residence was later known as the Green Lantern (Fig. 204). Shephard and Wheeler built it in 1896. It served as a crib before and after the Fattors owned it. Three girls worked out of this building. The building was torn down in the 1950's.

Fig. 204. **Then**-1954 photo of the 1896 crib that was later the Fattor's residence. In the
1920's, it was a three-girl crib known as the Green Lantern. (Ruth Gregory photo)

South of the Green Lantern is the two-story frame Zanoni-Pedroni Florence Saloon (Figs. 205 & 206), the present Bent Elbow Restaurant. This building stands on the site of one of Silverton's oldest and largest building, built by F. O. Sherwood in 1883. Absolutely nothing was ever written in the papers about this building. Since there were about one hundred and thirty prostitutes at work in Silverton at that time, it was probably a bordello. By 1889, the building was gone, either burned or moved.

In 1905, Ernest Zanoni, a native of Florence, Italy, purchased the land. He sold a half interest to his friend, Louis Pedroni. Construction began on their new Florence Saloon in the fall of 1907. The Florence Saloon was never a bordello. The saloon was on the main floor. The upstairs was used as a boarding house for miners.

Zanoni and Pedroni had a falling out, which resulted in Zanoni filing a lawsuit against Pedroni in Florence, Italy. The lawyers on both sides knew they had two "rich" Americans to deal with and purposely dragged out the lawsuit over a period of years. Zanoni finally won, but after paying the lawyers, he had nothing to show for his efforts.

Ernest Zanoni was also a miner. He obtained leases on several rich mining properties. At one time he had twenty men working for him. In 1921, Ernest retired to his native Italy with $250,000, a fortune at that time.

Ernest left the property to his son Lecio, pronounced Lee-Chay-O. When Lecio was a small boy, none of his friends could pronounce his name and he became known as "Leach" for the rest of his life. Leach owned the property until 1930, when he could no longer pay the taxes. The county became the owner of the old building until 1946 when R. M. Andreatta bought it at a tax sale. Andreatta let the taxes lapse again and ownership went back to the county. Frank Bostock paid $1,849 for back taxes and became the new owner.

The late Effie Andreatta bought the property after their Bent Elbow Restaurant burned in 1968. The Andreatta family sold the property in the spring of 1999.

Fig. 205. **Then**-1954 photo showing the 1907 Florence Saloon and Boarding House. (Ruth Gregory photo)

Fig. 206. **Then**-1909 panoramic view of Blair Street showing the 1907 Florence Saloon and the Union Boarding House. The Ore Bucket Gift Shop occupies the site of the old boarding house. (Eddie Lorenzon photo)

Fig. 207. **Now**-May, 1999 photo of the old 1907 Florence Saloon and Boarding House. Now the Bent Elbow Restaurant. (Allan G. Bird photo)

On the corner, next door to the Florence Saloon, was the Union Boarding House (Fig. 206), operated by Mrs. Mahoney. It was probably built about 1907. According to John Matties, it later became the Hood Boarding House. Joe Tamaselli purchased the building in May, 1924 and used it as a combined residence and boarding house for miners. He operated until the late 1930's or early 1940's. The building was demolished in the late 1950's. The Ore Bucket Gift Shop occupies the site today, 1999.

Prostitution ended on Blair Street in 1948, when "Jew" Fanny left for Salida. The district had such a bad name that the citizens who lived south of 11th Street, voted to change the name to Empire Street, which is the official name today for that portion of the street.

The following photo is of the man for whom Blair Street was named, Tom Blair. He came to Silverton to help build the Little Giant Mill in 1873. He was a millwright and carpenter by trade. He was one of the founding fathers of Silverton and owned a large portion of the town lots, which he helped to lay out. He made good money in the Aspen Mine north of town but decided to go into the saloon business, where he lost most of it. Tom Blair remained in Silverton until the Alaskan Gold Rush. He, and several friends, headed north to Alaska. A premature report of his death in the cold waters of the Yukon River reached Silverton. However, the report proved to be untrue. He never returned to Silverton.

Fig. 208. **Then**-Tom Blair, one of the founding fathers of Silverton, for whom Blair Street was named. (Mike Andreatta photo)

THE END

LIST OF ILLUSTATIONS

Page

ILLUSTRATIONS CONT'D

ILLUSTRATIONS CONT'D

ILLUSTRATIONS CONT'D

ILLUSTRATIONS CONT'D

Page

ILLUSTRATIONS CONT'D

Page

Page 182

ILLUSTRATIONS CONT'D

ILLUSTRATIONS CONT'D

ILLUSTRATIONS CONT'D

Page

Bibliography

Many of the stories in this book were gleaned from the old Silverton newspapers: The *La Plata Miner*, the *Silverton Democrat*, the *San Juan Herald*, and the *Silverton Standard & the Miner*.

San Juan County Courthouse and Silverton Town Hall records were gleaned for much of the property information.

Many of the stories were from personal interviews of the people cited in the book.

Bird, Allan G. Bordellos of Blair Street-Revised Edition. Advertising, Publications & Consultants, 444 Bass Lake Road, Pierson, MI 49339. June 1, 1993.

Bird, Allan G. The Grand Imperial Hotel Story, Allan G. Bird Publishing Co. 1135 Dudley St. Lakewood, CO 80215- May, 1995.

Bird, Allan G. Silverton Gold. Allan G. Bird Publishing Co., 1135 Dudley St. Lakewood, CO 80215.

Masterson, W. B. (Bat). Famous Gun Fighters of the Western Frontier. Vista Books, 1996. 0637 Blue Ridge Road, Silverthorne, CO 80498-8931

Nossaman, Allen. Many More Mountains, Vol. 3: Rails into Silverton. Sundance Publications Ltd. 250 Broadway, Denver, Colorado 80203. April, 1998.

INDEX

C

INDEX

INDEX

Ogsbury, David Clayton "Clate."
21, 24, 52, 68,
Old Town Square. 145
Olson, Tom. 151
Olympic Saloon. 12, 30, 31, 33, 40
O'Neil, John. 16
Opera House. 84, 115
Ore Bucket Gift Shop. 176
Orella, John. 164, 167
Orella, Pete. 94, 118, 165, 167
Ouray, Chief. 2
Outdoor Life Magazine. 125
Outdoor World Sport Shop. 46, 48
Oxford Beer Depot. 115

P

Packer, Alfred. 44
Palace Hall. 167, 168
Papadakis, J. & Co. 111
Parcel, Lew. 134
Parlor Gift Shop. 111
Pasco, Dr. 52, 53, 115
Patterson Bros. Livery. 88, 98, 128
Pearce & Reynold's Saloon. 100
Pearl, "21." 134, 153
Pearson Brothers. 84
Pearson Bros. Meat Market. 16, 84
Pearson, Robert. 126
Pedroni, Louis. 174
Pendleton & Hamlin. 16,
Penney, J. C. 134
Perrung & Akkola. 76
Perrung building. 125, 134
Perrung, John. 101
Pest House. 133
Pickle Barrel Restaurant. 7, 10, 13,
16, 25, 85, 97
Piemonte Saloon & Boarding House.
157, 158, 159
Piemonte, Italy. 143
Pierce, Mable. 147
Pile, George & Co. 30
Pile, Gov. Wm. 1
Pitman, Dr. E. T. 13
Plantz, T. P. 6
Plunket & Cleary. 68
Poodle Dog Saloon. 13, 15

Porter, J. A. 6
Posey & Wingate building. 4, 5, 15,
16, 20, 22, 68, 71, 79, 82, 97,
110, 111, 118, 119
Posey & Wingate Hardware Store.
21,
Posey , Wingate & Heffron
Hardware Store. 49
Post Office. 4, 6, 20, 28, 71, 79, 80,
85, 86, 131, 134
Presby, Dr. 53
Professor Shutterbug's Old Tyme
Photo Studio. 144
Prohibition. 71, 97, 122, 132, 156,
159, 165
Prosser, H. G. 78, 103
Prosser's Furniture & Undertaking
Parlor. 103
Pyle, Flora & Orville. 25

Q

Quong Wah. 74

R

R & J Restaurant. 73
Railroad Blockade. 63, 64, 139, 140,
141, 142, 157
Rainbow Route Garage. 132
Randall & Adsit. 4
Rawley, Francis. 165
Red Ashes Saloon. 159
Red Light District. 143, 148
Red Mountain Railroad. 77
Red Mountain Town. 50, 52, 71
Reed, John. 6
Reed, Mrs. 73
Reese Ball. 46
Reese, Dempsey. 1, 2, 4, 79
Reese Hook & Ladder Co. 9
Reese's Cabin. 4
Rew, Charlie. 121
Rexall Drug Store. 111, 128, 134
Roberts, E. L. 145
Roberts, Emma. 163

INDEX